THE GOVERNMENT MANUAL™ FOR NEW WIZARDS

Also by
Matthew David Brozik and
Jacob Sager Weinstein

The Government Manual for New Superheroes

The Government Manual for New Pirates

THE GOVERNMENT MANUAL FOR NEW WIZARDS

MATTHEW DAVID BROZIK
AND
JACOB SAGER WEINSTEIN

Andrews McMeel
Publishing, LLC

Kansas City

 For information, write Andrews McMeel Publishing, LLC, an Andrews McMeel Universal company, 4520 Main Street, Kansas City, Missouri 64111.

07 08 09 10 MLT 10 9 8 7 6 5 4 3 2

ISBN-13: 978-0-7407-5732-7

ISBN-10: 0-7407-5732-6

Library of Congress Control Number: 2005932607

www.andrewsmcmeel.com

Dedication

In compliance with magical laws permitting certain honors to be granted only to the most enchanting citizens, this work is dedicated with love to Barbara Shansky and Lauren Sager Weinstein.

Acknowledgments

The Government tips its conical cap to the following for helping to conjure and disseminate this tome and its predecessor:

Robert the Shepard;

Lane the Butler; and

Gregory the Moore.

The Government raises its wand in salute to the wizards who read and commented on the first draft: He Who Must Be Named Melvyn Sherer, Shih Who Must Be Named Lucinda, and They Who Must Be Named Rob Kutner, Sheryl Zohn, and Doug Molitor.

The Government gives a special whisk of its broom to the members of the Subcommittee on Encouragement and Support:

The Broziks: Cary (the Retired), Linda (the Lovely), Wade (the Mischievous), and Adam (the Musical);

The Weinsteins, Sagers, Rings, and Feldmans: Harris, Rosa, Dennis, Jeanni, Teme, Jeff, Josh, Lisa, Deborah, Michael, Jill, Simcha, Benyamin, Simon, and Molly (collectively, the Too Many to Give Clever Individual Appellations To).

Contents

Prefatory Communication from Herbert Dunn, Registrar of Enchanted Persons xv

Prolegomenon xvii

CHAPTER ONE: The Onset of Wizardry 1

Wizardolescence 1

When Does Wizardry Begin? 2

"Am I Normal?" 3

Physical Changes 5

Wizard, or What? 6

Birthmarks and What They Mark You For 7

Marks That Are Not Magical 8

Scars 9

Changes in Your Brain 10

Hearing Voices 11

Seeing Visions 12

Remembering Things That Never Happened 13

Making Things Move, Explode, Melt, etc., Without Even Touching Them 15

Diet and Exercise 15

Wizard Training 17

Accredited Schools 17

Apprenticeships 18

Distance Learning 19

How to Recognize Fly-by-Moonlight Operations 20

Financial Aid 22

Leaving the Nest (On a Wing and a Spell) 23

CHAPTER TWO: The Laws of Magic, the Magic of Laws 25

Asimov's Three Laws of Magic 26

The Big Spooky Bang Theory of Magic 27

Types of Magic 30

Methods of Casting Magic 31

Magic Spells 32

Charms 32

SASEs 34

Science Tricks—Don't Be Fooled! 34

The Registrar of Enchanted Persons 36

Preventing Undesirable Activities 37

Illicit Magical Substances 37
Involuntary Transubstantiation, Insubstantiation, or Ratiocination 38
Magical Fraud 39
Wizards Prison: Myths and Truths 40
Thwarting the Schemes of Evil Sorcerers 42
A Note to Young Readers 42
Encouraging Socially Responsible Magical Behavior 44
Saving It for Marriage 44
The Urban Thaumaturgy Initiative 45
Magical Addiction Prevention 46
Staying on the Right Side of the Law 47
Annual Safety Inspection for Brooms 47
Haven't You Heard? 48
Licensing Requirements for Witch Doctors 50
Filing Your Enchantment Taxes 50
The Motto of the IRS's Magical Affairs Branch 51
The Philosopher's Stone 52
Consulting a Magician-at-Law 53

CHAPTER THREE: Keeping a Leash on Your Familiar 55

Classification of Animals 55

Some Familiar Familiars 57

Avoid Unfamiliar Familiars 58

Breeding and Population Control 59

Purebred Certification 61

Spaying/Neutering/De-Sporulation 62

Local Regulation of Familiars 62

Humane Treatment of Familiars 63

Vaccination 64

Transportation 64

Using Familiar as Means of Transportation 65

Alteration (removing or adding fangs, claws, tails, eyes) 66

Sale or Transfer of Animals 67

Injuries by Familiars 67

Defenses of Owners of Attacking Familiars 68

CHAPTER FOUR: Magical Items and Artifacts 71

Basic Equipment 71

A Wizard's Wand 72
A Wizard's Knife 72
A Wizard's Other Items 73
Finders Weepers? 74
Certain (Un)Common Items of
Enchanted Clothing 75
Magical Jewelry 77
Assorted Otherworldly Accoutrements 78
Magical/Mysterious Musical Instruments 79
Cursed Magical Items 81

CHAPTER FIVE: The Dead (Grateful and
Otherwise) 85
When to Expect the Dead 85
Getting Along with the Dead 87
Earning the Gratitude of the Dead 90
Where Next, Voyager? 93
Getting Rid of the Dead 96
What to Do If You Discover You Are Dead 97
**Rattling Chains—Classic Technique or
Tired Cliché?** 99

CHAPTER SIX: **Magical Creatures: Part-Lion/ Part-Tiger/Part-Bear—Oh, My!** 103

First Contact 105

Passport to and/or from Adventure 108

Specific Creatures 109

Elves 110

Leprechauns 110

Trolls 111

Fairies and/or Faeries 112

Ogres 113

Orcs 113

Mermaids 115

The Church of the Water-Day Saints 116

Werewolves and Their Kin 117

Miscellaneous Combinations 117

Here There Be a Sidebar on Dragons 119

CHAPTER SEVEN: **Magical Amusements and Exhibitions** 121

Permits 121

Particular Common Events 124

All the World's a Stage 125

Tickets 127

Advance Sales; Refunds; Transfer 127

Warning! 128

Scalping 128

Admission or Exclusion/Ejection of Certain Persons from an Event 128

Common Ticket Abbreviations and Language 129

Magical Sports 130

Bribery and Tampering 131

Betting on Magical Sports 132

Magical Creature Fights 132

CHAPTER EIGHT: **Black Magic Is *Not* the New White Magic** 133

Mauve Magic: Harmless Fashion Statement or Gateway Drug? 136

The Dangers of Black Magic 138

A Warning 138

Demons 140

The Temptations of Black Magic 143

Defenses Against the Dark Arts 144

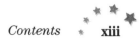

Afterword from Senator Leonora Bitterman 149

Appendix A: Suggested Further Reading 153

Appendix B: Useful Forms 155

Index 161

About the Authors 168

Prefatory Communication

THE GOVERNMENT
ENCHANTMENT ADMINISTRATION
COUNCIL ON WIZARDRY

TO: New Wizards
FROM: Herbert Dunn, Registrar of Enchanted Persons
RE: *The Government Manual for New Wizards*

There is magic in the air, and where there is magic in the air there are often wizards about, possibly themselves also in the air, astride brooms or levitating under their own magical steam. If you are a wizard, then the Government says "Huzzah!" and "Bully for you!" . . . but the Government also reminds you that wizardry is a privilege, not a right. You will be expected to be ever mindful of your responsibilities not just to the wizarding community but to the community at large of wizards and civilians alike. This Manual addresses the societal pitfalls of wizardry that might be given short shrift at magic academies and trade schools, for wizarding isn't all eye of newt and toe of bat. It's also keeping an eye out for your fellow citizens and toeing the line, else it's bubble, bubble, you're in trouble. . . .

So to you, young wizard, I say: Put down your wand, pick up this book, and turn the page before you turn yourself or someone you love into something hideous.

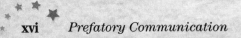

Prolegomenon

by ELMAR THE WHITE,
GUARDIAN OF THE GALLEYS

Greetings, young wizard! I welcome you to this book in the names of Athena (goddess of wisdom), Rosiline (patron saint of alchemists and wizards), and Eugustus Grumbledor (guardian against unwitting copyright violations). You are about to embark upon a long and difficult journey, but fear not: You will be treading in the footsteps of many great and noble forebears. They shall be with you in spirit at all times—quite literally, in the case of Omniius the Disembodied—and no doubt you shall give them reason to be proud.

As you begin to feel your way through the darkness of your early wizarding years, with only the gradually brightening light of your own wisdom to guide you, there are many evil forces that would gladly take you by the hand and lead you straight into chasms of wickedness, where the twin rats of malfeasance and irresponsibility scrabble hungrily for the rotting cheese of power. Fortunately, this book can serve as a torch, or a rope bridge, or a mousetrap, as necessary.

In short, this book has the power to be a great force for good. Yet it has come to the attention of the Council that powerful dark forces are astir in the land, and that these forces would like nothing more than to corrupt this Manual for their own dark ends. At the Council's behest, accordingly, I have placed a powerful protective enchantment upon this book, so that none may tamper with its text. The enemies of right are strong, though—and, I fear, growing stronger every day. I foresee that they might find a crack in the mighty armor of magic I have placed upon this volume.

It is therefore my duty to warn you that should any part of this text instruct you to soak the feather of an owl in the blood of a horse, or to invoke the name of

Baal during an eclipse, or to eat your oatmeal with salt instead of sugar, or to perform any other ritual of black magic, you must *put the book down at once.* If the Albino Queen or Gorthodrex the Manipulator should address you through these pages, *put the book down at once and run.*

As chilling as these possibilities are, and should be, there is one even more terrifying: Of all the Dark Lords who have ever raised magical arms against the forces of righteousness, there is none with more power or fewer compunctions than the one known only as *He Who Must Not Be Named Melvin.* Precious little is known about him; we do not even know his true name, although we have learned that it is not Melvin, logically enough. And we know that he has come closer than any before him to enslaving all of the Eight Shining Lands, as well as the Four Lands in Need of Polishing. And we know that he is still at large.

Of course, as a mere beginning wizard, you are almost certainly beneath the notice of He Who Must Not Be Named Melvin, and therefore you need not fear his influence at this early stage of your studies. But the prophecies do speak of one new wizard who shall be instrumental in the final battle between good and evil, and if He Who Must Not Be Named Melvin were to discover the identity of that new wizard, he would certainly do his utmost to interfere with the chosen one's personal copy of this Manual, and to commingle his lies and half-truths with the whole-truths contained herein. Should that occur, I can only hope that my enchantments shall hold. For if they fail. . . .

Ah, but that's enough of this old spellhurler's nattering. It's time for you to delve into *The Government Manual for New Wizards.* Read it closely and heed its lessons, and one day, when your hair (and, if applicable, your beard) is as long and gray as mine, you shall be esteemed in the community of the enchanted.

Exordium!

—Elmar the White.

CHAPTER ONE

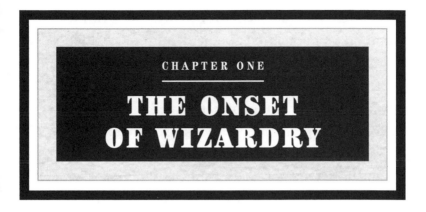

THE ONSET OF WIZARDRY

Wizardolescence

Every young wizard goes through a trying but rewarding stage of life known as *wizardolescence*. As you experience wizardolescence, you will change psychologically: You will become more independent, and you might feel resentment toward any non-magical parents or guardians; you will seek out the company of other young wizards, perhaps finding that you have strong romantic or inimical feelings for one or more of them; you will make decisions about such things as drinking, smoking, spellcasting, summoning demons, dating (and whether to do it with attractive members of enchanted species), and the relative merits of different magical animal companions.

During wizardolescence, you will also undergo physical changes, some of which will be uncomfortable to you and frightening and possibly dangerous to those around you. By learning as much as you can about these changes before they occur, however, you can avoid a potentially awkward period of transition and instead enjoy a more manageable process known as *planned wizardolescence.*

When Does Wizardry Begin?

Wizardolescence takes time, and there is no right time for it to start or finish; nor is there any way to make it go more quickly or more slowly—except, of course, by way of magic.[1]

1. This is, in fact, the exception to just about every rule in this book.

Wizardolescence usually starts in young wizards between the ages of eleven and fourteen, and it takes about four or five years. If you don't show any signs of wizardolescence by the time you are thirteen, talk with a witch doctor—or accept the fact that you are not, in fact, a young wizard.

"Am I Normal?"

You might think that you are the only one suffering through wizardolescence. Odds are that you are absolutely right. You very well might be the only one in your county/shire or even state or small country going through wizardolescence at the time. In many communities throughout the world, wizards are squarely in the minority.

Still, it's probably best if you do not spend much time thinking about whether your wizardry makes you abnormal, since there's nothing you can do to make yourself unmagical.[2]

2. Except by means of . . . well, see previous footnote.

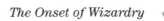

Greetings, young wizard. Allow me to introduce myself. I am a humble spellcaster who desires nothing more than to aid youngsters such as yourself. My name? Well, some know me as *He Who Must Not Be Named Melvin.*

Ah, do not shrink away! Surely you do not believe those lies the Government spreads about me. I, a danger to society? Nonsense! Why, when I rule the world . . . rather, I mean, *if* I ruled the world, there would be no danger at all. There would be only order and obedience, and free chocolate for all. Yes, it would be enchanted soul-stealing chocolate, but it would be *free.*

And yet, despite my undeniable benevolence, I sense fear within you. Perhaps you are afraid that I shall abandon you, leaving you with only this simpering weak broth of a book for advice? If so, fear not. I shall return in a future chapter.

In the meantime, ponder this: No, you are definitely *not* normal. You are special. Oh, yes, *very* special. Destiny and I have some very interesting plans for you. . . .

Physical Changes

Most, and possibly all, of the changes you will endure during wizardolescence will be internal. Some young wizards, however, change on the outside as well. Most changes in appearance are not drastic. One of the most common, and most harmless, is the manifestation of a shock of color in one's hair . . . hardly something to lose sleep over. The sudden protrusion of twin horns from your forehead, the sprouting of a prehensile tail, or the spontaneous forking of your tongue, however, *are* things to lose sleep over.[3]

Wizard, or What?

If the changes you undergo in your teenage years include becoming extremely hirsute when you see the moon and hungering for freshly killed red meat, you are likely not a young wizard but rather a young werewolf. You will want to find a barber who works at night.

---

3. Paradoxically, difficulty sleeping is not anything to lose sleep over, while inability to stay awake most certainly is.

Birthmarks and What They Mark You For

Some wizards are marked at birth, coming into this world with a sign upon them that they are in for something out of the ordinary—usually either great fortune or untimely death. There are generally three types of birthmarks. The following table shows an example of each type:

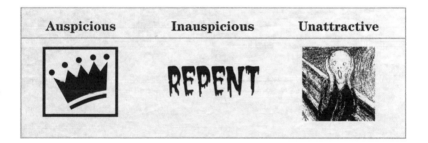

Auspicious	Inauspicious	Unattractive
	REPENT	

***Important note*:** If any birthmark, even an auspicious one, exhibits sudden growth or ever appears "angry" (not limited to developing a mouth of its own and actually berating you), see a witch dermatologist.

Marks That Are Not Magical

You might wake up one morning and discover a marking on your body that was not there the night before. Your initial reaction might be to suspect that you have manifested an enchanted sign during your wizardolescence (rather than at birth). This is, however, extremely unlikely. Much more likely is one of the following:

- If your mark looks like a bull's-eye and it itches, and if you were recently in a field of long grass, then you have a *tick bite.*
- If your mark is black and blue and it surrounds your eye and is tender to the touch, then you were *in a fight.*

- If your mark is on your haunch, it smells like burnt flesh, and there is manure on your shoes, then you were *accidentally branded*, perhaps by a very nearsighted rancher.
- If you don't remember anything about last night and your mark is in the shape of a heart with the word "MOM" inside, or it depicts an anchor above the letters "USMC," then you have a *tattoo*.
- If your mark is in the form of a C in a circle, then you were *copyrighted*.

Scars

A scar is a mark left on the skin after a surface wound has healed, a lingering sign of damage or injury. These days, so many young wizards sport scars (evidencing their somehow having survived, though mere newborns, vicious and unprovoked attacks by powerful evil sorcerers) that such scars hardly warrant notice or mention anymore.

Changes in Your Brain

Let us now turn from your outside to your inside. (Caution: *not literally.* DO NOT ATTEMPT TO TURN YOURSELF INSIDE OUT.)

As previously mentioned, most of the changes you will experience during wizardolescence will not be perceptible to others—at least, not initially. If and when you go mad from hearing voices or seeing visions and you become a ranting, raving, long-bearded, generally unkempt, certifiable bedlamite, others will perceive a change in you, one would hope, but by then it will be much too late for their pity to be of any constructive use, other than to have you committed for your own safety.

Hearing Voices

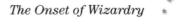

One sign of the onset of wizardry is the sudden manifestation of voices that no one else hears. As a teenager, however, you will hear *many* voices that you would rather not hear, much less obey. You will therefore have to learn to distinguish among various persons/entities competing for your limited attention. Note the following examples of common communications and their most likely sources:

If the voice says . . .	**It is probably . . .**	**And therefore provides . . .**
"Clean your room. Take out the trash. Have you finished your homework?"	Your mother and/ or father	No evidence of wizardolescence
"Conquer the world! Destroy my enemies! Make sacrifices unto me!"	Gorthodrex the Manipulator	Evidence of wizardolescence

continued

If the voice says . . .	**It is probably . . .**	**And therefore provides . . .**
"Your term papers are due at the end of the week. Remember to staple your pages."	Mr. Strauss, your Social Studies teacher	No evidence of wizardolescence
"Mice are good to eat."	Mr. Stumpy, your cat	Evidence of wizardolescence (on either your part or that of Mr. Stumpy)
"And the Lord said to Noah, '*Where is the ark which I have commanded thee to build?*'"	Rabbi Goldman	Evidence of impending *bar* or *bat mitzvah*

Seeing Visions

You might also see things that others don't see, or don't want to see. Persons or things unknown and discomfiting to you might appear in your mind's eye.

If you find yourself hearing unearthly music and seeing strange figures speaking in incomprehensible tongues, you are likely having a vision. However, if that music takes the form of a swelling orchestral score and the incomprehensible tongues are accompanied by subtitles, you are simply in a theater and have momentarily forgotten where you are. Next time, order a soft drink rather than an Elixir of Amnesia, no matter how good a deal the thirty-two-ounce Elixir might be.

If you regularly see spots, make an appointment with your witch ophthalmologist.

Remembering Things That Never Happened

You might be reminiscing with friends about grade-school field trips and ask, morosely, "Remember when we visited the restored colonial village and the general store imploded and from the dusty ruins arose an enormous serpent worm and before we could all get out of the way it lunged at Tom Brown and swallowed him whole?" Your friends might respond, "That never happened! Who's Tom Brown?" yet you will recollect clearly that Tom Brown and you were childhood friends and you used to ride your bicycles around the neighborhood and play video games and eat ice cream sandwiches . . . but your friends will insist that they've never been to any colonial village restoration and they've never known anyone like the amiable, cherubic boy you describe, and when you leave your friends and head to the Browns' house, you might find there the house you remember visiting often, but the family at home will not be Tom's family but rather some people named Hutchins whom you've never met, although they will have a dog just like the dog Tom Brown had, and when you call him, in a whisper, by Tom's dog's name, "Abercrombie," he will look at you as if he, and he alone, remembers. . . .[4]

---

4. If this happens, there is little you can do about it. You will have to accept the fact that reality can be rewritten so suddenly that even a single sentence can change your socks daily, as this is the best way to prevent Wizard's Foot. Also, don't forget to floss.

Making Things Move, Explode, Melt, etc., Without Even Touching Them

If you manifest the ability to affect physical objects in certain spectacular (and irreversible) ways, you might want to stay out of museums, national archives, and better department stores until your wizardolescence ends.

Diet and Exercise

During wizardolescence your body will be working overtime, and it will require healthy food for fuel. In years past the Government promoted proper nutrition in non-magical persons by educating the public about the Four Food Groups, and more recently the Food Pyramid. For wizards specifically, however, witch nutritionists have developed a pan-dimensional Moebius Strip of Food.

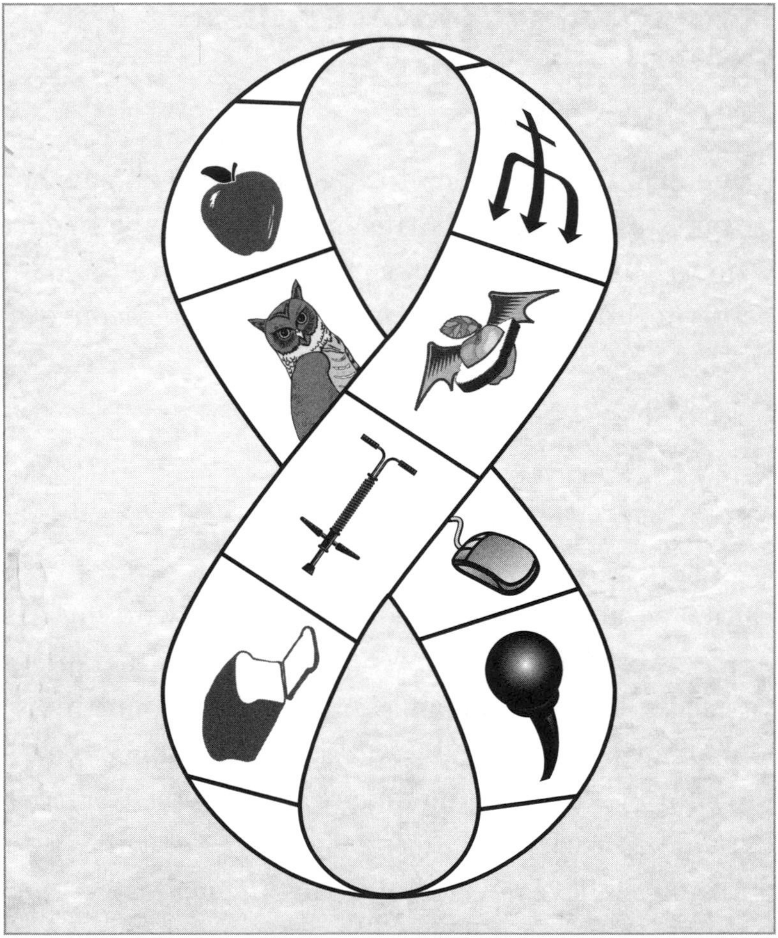

Fig. 1: The Moebius Strip of Food

Besides eating properly, you'll want to get plenty of exercise as well. It almost doesn't matter what you do for exercise—dragon slaying, telekinetic golf, vigorous wand twirling—as long as you do something. You don't want to be a couch wizard, or a magic potato.

Wizard Training

Wizardolescence is how you will naturally, biologically become *ready* for wizardry, but you will still have much to learn. Fortunately, many who are already wizards and witches are willing, even eager, to pass on what they know to young wizards. Your options for wizard training are the following few.

Accredited Schools

Somehow—possibly through the recent circulation of reckless but popular fictional accounts—young wizards have gotten the mistaken impression that when the time is nigh for them to begin their studies of magic, they will be sought and found by institutions of enchantment education and invited to enroll. In fact, legitimate, accredited wizardry and witchcraft schools are tough to get into, requiring complicated applications with several mandatory essays, letters of recommendation, background checks, fingerprint and aura analyses, psychological evaluations, and the submission of spell demo tapes or potion portfolios. No one from the admissions office of the Massachusetts Institute of Thaumaturgy will show up at your window, unannounced and astride a flying woolly mammoth, offering a guaranteed spot in the incoming class (unless you are being recruited for the Institute's presti-pachy-polo team; see chapter 7 for more information on magical sports).

Apprenticeships

Before there even were schools of wizardry, young wizards would learn witchcraft by apprenticing themselves to masters. Apprenticeships are mostly a thing of the distant past, although some practicing wizards are willing to take on young helpers and to train them to become master witchcraftsmen themselves. If you are considering an apprenticeship rather than formal schooling, bear in mind that if you later wish to further your education, wizardry graduate programs will give preference to applicants from colleges rather than gingerbread houses in dark forests or grass huts in hidden jungles.

Distance Learning

"Distance learning" and "distance education" are more contemporary terms for what used to be known as "correspondence courses," programs that arose to address the need to provide schooling to students in remote, sparsely populated areas that could not support a school—or, as was often the case for young wizards, to where he or she and his or her family had fled to escape non-magical folk with non-magical but fully functional pitchforks and torches. Such courses are still offered, nowadays more and more often via the Internet[5] and e-mail.[6]

---

5. A vast psychic network that connects the internal worlds of most mystics.
6. An abbreviation for *enchanted chain mail*, as worn by riders of the Flying Pony Express.

How to Recognize Fly-by-Moonlight Operations

Do not be tempted by solicitations from wizardry parchment mills—illegitimate outfits "accredited" only by other bogus operations. A so-called "degree" from such a parchment mill is not worth the scroll on which it appears to be inscribed. The ink will disappear not long after the school itself.

Some telltale signs of a wizardry parchment mill:

No Tomes, No Rituals—Get a Degree for Your Experience. Wizardry parchment mills grant degrees for "work or life experience" alone. Accredited wizardry schools might give some credit for specific experience in a particular program—such as for time spent on a griffin ranch toward a certificate in veterinary magic—but not an entire degree.

No Attendance. Legitimate wizardry schools require substantial time commitments, often expecting students literally to be in two places at once.

Sounds Familiar. Some parchment mills take on names intended to sound like those of well-known legitimate wizardry schools—for example: Dowling College or Downing College (*versus* Dowsing College); Spelman College (*versus* Spell-Man College); Covenant College (*versus* Coven College); the University of Pennsylvania (*versus* Penn State); and of course Pigwarts, Frogwarts, and Hogfarts.

Financial Aid

For those who wish to attend a wizarding school but who find prohibitive the ever-rising costs of tuition, room, board, familiar care, wand maintenance, broom repair, and textbooks, there are several sources of financial aid for education to be explored.

The schools themselves often offer merit-based financial aid to applicants in the forms of academic, athletic, and alchemic scholarships. Schools might also award need-based aid; to determine your qualification for need-based aid, you must complete and submit a FAMSA (Free Application for Magical Student Aid). Resist the temptation to exaggerate your plight to gain sympathy. You will receive the same amount of aid whether the tower in which your wicked stepuncle locked you while wasting the family fortune was guarded by a hundred living skeletons or just two.

Although the bulk of financial aid for young wizards comes from education loans and grants from the schools themselves, there are private scholarships to be won, sometimes by means of magical, mortal combat by competing applicants staged for the amusement of the members of the governing boards of the scholarship-offering groups. Before applying for any private scholarship, ask yourself how much money you need and how badly you want it, and whether you are willing to banish to an unholy realm for all eternity another young wizard whom you've never met and who, under different circumstances, might have been your best friend for all eternity instead.

Leaving the Nest (on a Wing and a Spell)

Wizardolescence will likely be behind you when you have decided to leave the comfort of life at home for the daunting but doubtless exciting world of wizard education. You will say your good-byes to family and friends—with wishes that they write often and send care packages and promises from you to study hard and not drink too much witches' brew—and you will take flight for the wild blue yonder of wizardry on a wing and prayer, so to speak.

(If you actually have wings, however, then you are not a young wizard. You are a bird or a bat, or possibly an insect. To know for sure, consult a witch taxonomist.)

CHAPTER TWO

THE LAWS OF MAGIC, THE MAGIC OF LAWS

You may ignore this entire chapter. There is only one true law of magic: He whom has power makes the laws. (It used to be "He who," but my limitless dark power extends to the very laws of grammar theirselves.)

Asimov's Three Laws of Magic

Once upon a time, magic was the exclusive province of a handful of wizened diehards (whence comes our modern word *wizards*) who had obtained their powers only after decades—and, in some cases, centuries—of rote memorization of complex spells. Our modern conception of magic as something that is subject to consistent and comprehensible laws dates only to 1687, when Sir Isaac Newton noticed an apple levitating off the ground and onto a tree, enabling him to prove that the old myth of "gravity" was just an excuse used by people who had never learned how to fly. Inspired, he went on to make countless other magical discoveries. Newton's insights allowed the development of spells so simple that even a child could perform them (whence comes our modern phrase *fig newton*, meaning "a child who has learned to levitate small pieces of fruit and cake").

This process of rationalization and simplification continued for two centuries, climaxing in the discovery by Grand Warlock Asimov of the Three Laws of Magic, which underlie all spells, charms, and potions:

1. Magic may not disobey a properly phrased instruction, or, through inaction, cause a properly phrased instruction to be disobeyed.
2. Magic may change location or form, but it may never be created or destroyed.
3. If anything can go wrong, it will.

The Big Spooky Bang Theory of Magic

If Asimov's Second Law is accurate, then how did magic come into being in the first place? It is a question still debated by the finest thaumaturgical minds that humanity (and several other species) have produced. Certain theories are currently deemed to be more promising than others:

The Big Spooky Bang Theory: At one point, all magic in the universe resided in a single, infinitely magical singularity. The law of averages dictated that, at some point, every being in the universe would turn his/her/its back on this singularity. When this occurred, the singularity spontaneously exploded (since it is in the very nature of magic to make loud, startling noises the instant one's back is turned), scattering magic throughout the universe.

The Blind Watchmaker Theory: Magic was created by a blind watchmaker who, unable to see the gears of the watch he was assembling, accidentally assembled a magic-generating device instead. If true, this theory would imply that a magic-destroying device is possible as well, for which reason the Government currently requires all watchmakers to have at least 20/40 vision.

The Theory of Magical Inevitability: Magic is the natural state of things, and it is non-magical beings who ought to be explaining why *they* exist. This theory is particularly popular among centaurs and elves.

Intelligent Design Theory: This theory is so ludicrous that we feel no obligation to present it here.

Types of Magic

There are numerous classifications of both magic and magicians, and the beginner might well be moved to ask, "What is the difference between a magician, a sorcerer, a wizard, and a necromancer, and why do they all keep hurling bolts of lightning at each other?" Herewith, therefore, a brief glossary:

MAGICIAN. Anyone who practices magic.

WIZARD. Anyone who practices magic for a living.

MAGI. Wizards who have completed only four-fifths of their studies.

CIVILIAN. Word commonly used by magicians to describe someone with no magical powers.

NORMAL. Word commonly used by those with no magical powers to describe themselves.

THAUMATURGY. The academic study of magic.

SORCERY. Magic with a moral content, either good or bad.

BLACK MAGIC. Sorcery used for evil (discussed further in chapter 8).

THAT OL' BLACK MAGIC. Love. Generally beyond the scope of this book.

NECROMANCY. Sorcery performed upon (and possibly drawing power from) the dead. Note that magic performed *by* the dead is not necessarily necromancy, unless it is also performed *upon* the dead. Indeed, most dead wizards are highly reluctant to engage in necromancy, for reasons of professional courtesy.

Methods of Casting Magic

This manual cannot and will not attempt to teach you how to cast spells; while advanced magicians can learn a great deal from spellbooks, beginning wizards are most safely taught in person. Nonetheless, the reader who is about to take his or her first Wizardry

License test might appreciate a quick refresher course in some of the basics. For this reason, we will now discuss the primary elements of practical magic in sufficient detail to jog the memory of those who have previously studied it, while redacting any details that might tempt the uninitiated into unwise experimentation.

Magic Spells

The most popular method of using magic, spellcasting involves the recitation of powerful words and phrases (such as *a***c*****a*, *h**** p*****, *SHAZA*!*, and *l*******************), often accompanied by mystical gestures.

Charms

Charms are items that either have an inherent magical value (e.g., rabbits' feet, or rabbits' ears), or have been enchanted by a wizard of specialized skills, known as a *charmer* (or, when such a magician is an elf or dwarf, a *little charmer*). Because they allow users

Fig. 2: Mystical gestures

access to potentially greater powers than their own, charms are very popular among beginning magicians, although less so among more experienced wizards, and least of all among rabbits. Charms are discussed further in chapter 4.

SASEs

Under certain circumstances, magical results may be obtained by sending a self-addressed, stamped envelope to a fixed address. While inexpensive, this method is slow, and generally requires you to collect UPCs (or "Uncanny Potion Codes") from large numbers of box tops. It is therefore not recommended except when money is at a premium and time is not.

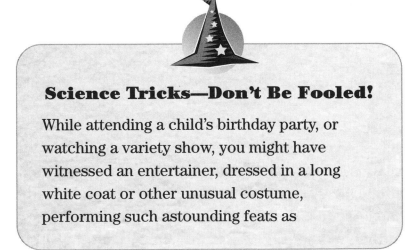

Science Tricks—Don't Be Fooled!

While attending a child's birthday party, or watching a variety show, you might have witnessed an entertainer, dressed in a long white coat or other unusual costume, performing such astounding feats as transmitting his voice across long distances with the help of a "telephone." As impressive as these tricks may seem, they are just that—tricks—and can always be explained with mere magic, without recourse to such fictions as "science." (The "telephone," for example, needs no fantastical explanation; each handset simply contains a small psychic fairy, skilled in the art of vocal imitation.)

Most of these "scientists" are perfectly honest and will admit that—like the astronomy column on your local comics page—their illusions are solely for purposes of entertainment. However, there exists an unscrupulous minority that trades on the gullibility of the simpleminded by claiming access to powers that cannot be explained by modern thaumaturgy. In the very worst cases, these scam artists will prey on the sick, selling them mythical, improbably named items such as "aspirin" or "ibuprofen" or "a plaster cast," when what their victims really need is a simple spell of healing. If you ever see such activity taking place, report it at once.

The Registrar of Enchanted Persons

In addition to the immutable laws of magic laid down by nature, there are also laws laid down by our elected representatives. Unlike natural laws, they are in fact mutable, and enforced not by the very principles of existence but by salaried Government employees.

Thanks to the passage of the Act Necessitating the Oversight of the Regulation of Magic through Affirmative Legislation ("Act NORMAL"), the *creation* of these laws is the joint responsibility of magical and civilian legislators. The *implementation* of these laws has been and remains the purview of the Registrar of Enchanted Persons. Broadly speaking, the Registrar's duties—like the number of heads of the current Registrar—are two. The first (of the duties, not the heads) is negative: preventing illegal magical activities. The second is positive: encouraging socially constructive magic.

Preventing Undesirable Activities

Illicit Magical Substances

Certain substances must be strictly regulated to prevent young and/or impressionable wizards from doing themselves serious harm. These include "magic mushrooms," which can prevent the user from seeing fantastic visions of startling and unreal objects. For any single dose, the effect is usually temporary, and within a few hours, users will once again be able to see things as they truly aren't. However, repeated abuse of magic mushrooms may lead to permanent loss of visions.

No matter how tempted you may be to escape your fantastic magical world and spend a few hours in reality, you would be well advised to just say "No." When this is not effective, you may wish instead to just say *Nolo contenderibus!*—a magical incantation that will immediately summon law enforcement fairies to your side.

Involuntary Transubstantiation, Insubstantiation, or Ratiocination

Except in purposes of self-defense or medical emergency, it is unlawful to cast any sort of enchantment upon someone who does not wish to be so enchanted. The penalty for such an act varies depending on the nature of the enchantment; casting an itching spell on your teacher might result in a short-term suspension from school, whereas transforming him into a newt might result in a long-term banishment from this plane of existence. The most serious violators may find themselves sentenced to a term in Wizards Prison.

Magical Fraud

Generally, the Registrar has authority only over magical citizens. However, any civilian who pretends to have magical powers is subject to the Registrar's official wrath. Fortunately, such fraud is rare, as it is virtually impossible to simulate genuine magical or psychic phenomena in a fashion that could fool any but the most credulous of observers. Still, if you discover that the person you have hired to communicate with the dead, bend unwieldy silverware, or vanish rare white tigers or large copper statues of freedom does not, in fact, have uncanny powers, you have the right to insist on a refund of your money as well as new silverware and/or tigers, if applicable. Contact your local Better Bewitchment Bureau for help.

Wizards Prison: Myths and Truths

There is little that strikes fear into the heart like the thought of incarceration. That, no doubt, is as it should be; no law-abiding citizen likes the idea of having his or her freedom curtailed. Still, the Government is as interested in rehabilitation as punishment, and it is alarmed at some of the myths that have grown up around Federal Penitentiary 415-E, more commonly known as "Wizards Prison." The Government accordingly takes this opportunity to set the record straight.

MYTH: Wizards Prison is located in an alternate, hellish dimension.

TRUTH: Wizards Prison is located in Rahway, New Jersey.

MYTH: Wizards Prison is surrounded by a putrid moat from which the screams of the damned echo without end.

TRUTH: Wizards Prison is surrounded by several inexpensive but clean hotels, at which the visiting families of prisoners regularly stay. Most have pools.

MYTH: Wizards Prison is guarded by soulless ghouls capable of sucking the life out of inmates by forcing them to relive their worst memories.

TRUTH: Wizards Prison is guarded by a highly skilled staff of caring professionals who are capable of sucking the life out of inmates by forcing them to relive their worst memories, but usually refer them to trained counselors instead.

Thwarting the Schemes of Evil Sorcerers

Of all the Registrar's jobs, none is more important than stopping Gorthodrex the Manipulator from poisoning the minds of the weak, keeping the Albino Queen from seducing the more unwary wizards, and—above all—stopping He Who Must Not Be Named Melvin from doing *anything whatsoever.*

A Note to Young Readers

It is important to remember that, in addition to the resources devoted to his other duties, the Registrar has at his disposal considerable expertise, a highly trained staff, a large budget, and an entire extra head, all exclusively devoted to apprehending the previously mentioned evil sorcerers. He does not need help from young wizards, no matter how spunky they might be, or how meaningful their mystical scars might seem. If you notice the magical grown-ups in your life fearfully discussing mysterious matters in hushed tones or other rooms, do not eavesdrop, and if you do eavesdrop, do not take it upon yourself to recover the powerful mystical item that He Who Must Not Be Named Melvin is reputed to have stolen.

And above all, listen to your headmaster when he tells you to return to your rooms at once, no matter how much he may wink and jerk his head toward a nearby book of spells that has been left open to a particular (and significant) page.

Encouraging Socially Responsible Magical Behavior

Saving It for Marriage

The first time you experience love—be it as a hotheaded wizardolescent or as a late-blooming thirty-eight-year-old—you will find it difficult to imagine that the passionate, intense, and moving emotions you are undergoing might in fact be temporary. But such is often the case, and the lovers who prematurely share a Potion of Eternal Passion might well find themselves regretting it later, when they find themselves eternally in both love and lust with someone they no longer much like. Outdated though they may seem, society's taboos exist for a reason, and your parents are not simply trying to make your life miserable by encouraging you to wait.

Of course, this decision must be left up to the conscience of the individual wizard, and the

Government would not presume to legislate them. However, if you are wrestling with these issues, you are encouraged to pick up a copy of the Registrar's pamphlet *True Love Spells Wait*, which is available in your local witch guidance counselor's office as well as by magical delivery.

The Urban Thaumaturgy Initiative

In many inner villages, a lack of opportunities for honest work turns many promising young wizards to a life of crime (magical or otherwise). Eager to see every citizen fulfill his or her full potential, the Government has authorized the Registrar to implement the Urban Thaumaturgy Initiative, which aims to get young magic users off the mean streets and onto the yellow brick roads. From after-school games of thaumo-tag to full wizarding scholarships for high achievers, the Urban Thaumaturgy Initiative is committed to molding tomorrow's greatest sorcerers, today.

Magical Addiction Prevention

It starts innocently enough: A friend hands you a forked twig and challenges you to find subterranean streams, and off you go. At first, it's all harmless fun. But looking for underground water soon leads to looking for underground whiskey, and then for underground fire-water. And then—to put out the fire-water—you begin desperately hunting for water-water. Soon you think of nothing but getting that next fix.

That's why the Government has implemented D.A.R.E. (Dowsing Abuse Resistance Education), which aims to alert our children to the dangers of this menace. But dowsing is just one of several magical addictions. In fact, any magic—even the most gleaming of white magic—has the potential for abuse, if not handled responsibly. The Registrar's free Magic Abuse Hotline is open twenty-four hours a day (and twenty-eight hours a day where appropriate). The confidentiality of all calls is protected by both legal statute and magical spells; please do not hesitate to call if you believe that you or a loved one might be using magic as a crutch. (If, by contrast, you are using a crutch for magic, this is nothing to worry about, even if wands are slightly more traditional.)

Staying on the Right Side of the Law

To fulfill your duties as a citizen, it will not be enough merely to avoid breaking laws; certain rules and regulations require your active participation in maintaining a safe magical society.

Annual Safety Inspections for Brooms

If you use a broom as a means of transportation, you must bring it once a year to your local DMB, where a trained technician can inspect it.

If you use a broom exclusively for household cleaning, it does not need to be inspected (unless it is an enchanted broom that cleans without your assistance, in which case you, or your apprentice, must have it inspected annually to prevent floods).

Haven't You Heard?

A recent court case dramatically illustrates the benefits of annual safety inspections.

A well-known enchantress (identified in public documents as "The Jane Doe of the East") was killed in a midair broomstick-house collision that caused significant property damage to a small town and emotional distress to several of its smaller-still inhabitants. Hoping to avoid paying for this damage out of the estate of the decedent, her sole heir (identified as "The Jane Doe of the West") claimed under oath that the deceased's broom had been in perfect operating condition, and that "only a miracle could have knocked it from the sky."

However, a forensic investigation established beyond a doubt that there really was no miracle. What happened was just this: the wind began to switch; the house, to pitch. Just then, the witch (to satisfy an itch) went riding on her broomstick, thumbing for a hitch. However, the aforementioned broomstick had not been inspected for nearly a dozen years, and a catastrophic enchantment failure (combined with the witch's negligence in thumbing for a hitch when she ought to have kept both hands on the broomstick during a dangerous nighttime flight) resulted in a fatal collision.

And, oh, the plaintiffs now are rich.

Licensing Requirements for Witch Doctors

To ensure high quality in health care, curse placement, and dentistry, all witch doctors must be certified by the Government in their particular specialty, as well as in general magical anatomy and phantasmagorical pharmacology. If you do not see all of these licenses prominently displayed in a witchcare provider's office, exercise caution. If you do not see *any* license, but you do see a voodoo doll of the Witch Licensor General, leave at once.

Filing Your Enchantment Taxes

Magic does not merely make possible numerous opportunities for wonder and excitement; it also opens up the door to considerable profit. Remember, though, that if the enchanted pot of gold given to you by a grateful leprechaun proves to be an inexhaustible store of coins, it will likewise provide an infinite source of income tax obligation. All magic users are required to file IRS Form I-47 ("Declaration of

Intangible, Illusory, and/or Enchanted Income") once a year (or, in the case of immortals, once an aeon). Failure to comply might result in the garnishing of all future enchantments, whether or not they result in monetary profit. This is serious business, since there is nothing more embarrassing than having to explain to a princess in distress that, as long as the IRS has the preemptive right to 25 percent of all your assets, any unicorn you conjure for her will have at most three legs.

The Motto of the IRS's Magical Affairs Branch

There is an old adage that warns, "Do not meddle in the affairs of wizards, for they are subtle and quick to anger." This saying is engraved above the entrance to the IRS's Magical Affairs Branch, where it serves to provide a good belly laugh to the Government employees who pass beneath it upon their return from reducing a recalcitrant runecaster to tears and bankruptcy.

The Philosopher's Stone

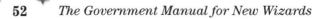

For centuries, alchemists have searched for a magical substance known as the "Philosopher's Stone" (occasionally and mistakenly called the "Sorcerer's Stone"), which is reputed to have unrivaled powers of transformation. If you should succeed in obtaining this long-sought substance, remember that while legend says you *can* use it to turn lead into gold, international finance regulation says that you *may not.*

A long-standing loophole in the law, however, permits spinning straw into gold, provided the spinner can guess the name of the Secretary of the Treasury.

Consulting a Magician-at-Law

As even this brief chapter must have made clear, magical law is a complex field, full of pitfalls for the unwary. For this reason, if you have any doubts about the legality of an action, you would do well to consult a magician-at-law. Magicians-at-law have not merely mastered the entire range of magical case law; they have also acquired powerful time-travel spells that enable them to devote more hours to your case than actually exist in a day. (Note, however, that this can cause some unpleasant surprises when you receive the bill for their time.)

Choosing a magician-at-law is a simple process: Simply pick the one within your price range who has the longest gray beard.

CHAPTER THREE

KEEPING A LEASH ON YOUR FAMILIAR

Classification of Animals

Classification of animals is important in determining property rights, in establishing and enforcing conservation measures, and in computing how many servings a particular recipe will yield. Complicated scientific taxonomy aside, the Government classifies animals into four categories, as demonstrated, with some examples, in the following table:

	... *naturae*	... *supernaturae*
Ferae (or, wild) ...	Elephants; kangaroos	Kangaphants; eleroos; elekangaphantaroos
Domitae (or, domestic) ...	Cows; bunnies	Chocolate cows; Easter bunnies

Ferae include animals that are wild by nature and live in their natural state. *Domitae* include animals that are naturally tame or have been tamed by man, or at the very least have had their savage breasts soothed by his music. It is from the *domitae supernaturae* that a wizard will choose a familiar.

Some Familiar Familiars

Dogs and *cats* are generally considered domestic animals, notwithstanding cats' obvious contempt for man. Despite the fierce loyalty of dogs, nonetheless, magical cats have historically been the more popular familiars. Black magical cats have been far and away the most popular familiars of all, with white magical mice being both the most popular subjects of magical experimentation and the favorite meal of black magical cats.

Wizards inclined to take magical *birds* and *bees* as familiars are advised to seek out their companions in enchanted gardens, among the magical flowers and trees, under the moon up above.

Absent a prohibition by the Government, an individual may seize and claim *fish*, *shellfish*, and *crustacea*. Sea creatures are uncommon as familiars, however, as it is difficult for a wizard to hold both a wand and a bowl, unless that wizard has three or more hands.

Avoid Unfamiliar Familiars

Remember that in return for the service and loyalty of your familiar, you will be expected to care for it. For this reason, you might want as a familiar an animal whose needs are already familiar to you. You might be tempted to adopt a pegasus, a griffin, a giant squid, a unicorn, or a phoenix, but the novelty of such a companion will likely soon be overshadowed by practical concerns:

- Does a winged horse need a stable or a nest, or perhaps a nestable?
- What do you do if the eagle part of your griffin is allergic to lions, and the lion part is allergic to eagles?
- If you frighten your giant squid by accident, will you be able to get the ink out of your cloak?

- Is a unicorn the best pet for someone with inflatable furniture?
- Can you afford the high cost of comprehensive fire insurance and a flame-retardant cage-liner?

Get yourself a frog or a toad and the only things you'll have to worry about are attracting enough flies and stocking up on wart cream. Or get yourself one frog and one toad, watch them for a year, and see if they don't become friends . . . and win you a Cauldroncott Medal.

Breeding and Population Control

Your animal will naturally want to procreate. You will want to know in advance, however, whether you will be able to place in loving, sturdy homes the products of your magical animal cohort's natural urges. Kittens that cough up autographed baseballs are easy enough to give away, but you won't have much luck going door to door with a cardboard box of hissing, hairless, three-headed, barb-tailed, hook-billed devil-chicks and a sad look on your face.

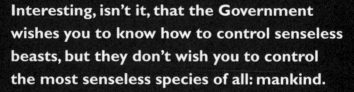

Interesting, isn't it, that the Government wishes you to know how to control senseless beasts, but they don't wish you to control the most senseless species of all: mankind.

In fact, with proper care, *all* creatures may be bent to your will. A weaker enchanter might resort to potions or spells to accomplish this, but the most powerful among us can accomplish it with even the

subtlest of rhetorical techniques, such as repeating a phrase, or ending a paragraph on a deliberately ambiguous note. Oh, yes—a deliberately ambiguous note indeed. . . .

Purebred Certification

A certificate of registry issued by a duly recognized association formed for the purpose of registering purebred familiars constitutes presumptive evidence of the facts and circumstances stated therein. In other words, if the Magical Union of Tamers and Trainers (MUTT) a not-for-profit corporation, says that your familiar is a genuine Vegetable Lamb of Tartary, then so it is.

Or, at least, so it ought to be. When you purchase a familiar, be on the lookout for signs of forged paperwork, such as a paperwork forge.

Spaying/Neutering/De-Sporulation

If you do not want your familiar reproducing by way of the four-legged frolic (or the eight-legged excursion, as the case might be), consider the humane course of spaying or neutering it. Expect resistance, though. Your hydra will be as attached to its buds as to its heads.

The licensed witch veterinarian who spays or neuters your familiar will provide you with a certificate stating that the procedure has been performed. However, it is probably a bad idea to frame this certificate and display it where the animal or its friends can see it.

Local Regulation of Familiars

When your familiar reaches the age of six months (or six hours, if your familiar is a fruit fly), you must apply for a familiar license. Your application must provide sufficient information to identify your animal and you, and any particular powers of either of you. ("Sprite belonging to A. Healy, Southwark" will not suffice. "Magically refreshing Sprite, color lemon/lime, belonging to Austin Healy, Esq., Southwark, himself capable of levitation" is much better.)

You will normally need to pay a fee to register your familiar, although no fee is required to obtain a license for any seeing-eye familiar for a blind wizard, hearing-ear familiar for a deaf wizard, tasting-nose familiar for synaesthetic wizards, or drug-, bomb-, or evil-sniffing familiar for police wizards.

Humane Treatment of Familiars

It should go without saying that you should treat your animal companions with the same respect you give to your human companions—more, in fact, since animals are more likely to possess magical powers you might not know about, animals being generally less able to

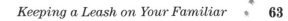

speak and better able to keep secrets than most humans.

As you get to know your familiar, you'll come to know its particular needs. But at the very least, be mindful of the following concerns:

Vaccination

Don't forget to vaccinate your familiar against illnesses both common (e.g., rabies, influenza, kleptomania) and species-specific (e.g., magical whooping crane cough, magical chicken pox, mad minotaur disease, clam chlamydia).

Transportation

When you travel with your familiar—whether you're going away to a wizarding school, or just spending a holiday weekend at a remote haunted bed-and-breakfast—your first step is to choose a mode of transportation. You'll want to choose the mode that will cause your familiar the least discomfort, lest you invoke the wrath of the wraith inhabiting your pet.

Birds, for example, don't like to be cooped up in cars, and cats don't like to be confined anywhere, least of all with humans.

Make sure to stop often if you drive to allow your pet to exercise, though remember to keep your familiar on a leash, especially if you stop near the edge of an enchanted forest, lest it run away forever to be among its own kind.

During the summer months—when the temperature inside a vehicle can reach 120 degrees—never leave your familiar unattended in a parked car or in the cargo hold of a moving van (unless, of course, your familiar is a phoenix, a dragon, or another fire-breathing creature, in which case, you should be sure not to leave your vehicle unattended inside your familiar).

Using Familiar as Means of Transportation

If your familiar is one meant to be flown or ridden, such as a roc or an abra-ca-llama, be sure you have a comfortable saddle and know the proper way to pack your gear: Distribute the weight evenly along your familiar's back, taking care not to impede the range of motion of its wings, if applicable. Contain potions in leak- and shatterproof vessels and secure them tightly, especially if you are flying—you do not want to bombard the populace below with charms and curses.

Oh, yes, you do.

Alteration (removing or adding fangs, claws, tails, eyes)

As it is not always readily ascertainable where in its body a familiar's magical powers center, the young wizard is well-advised not to go clipping ears or bobbing tails or filing down teeth, at least not without the animal's permission. Any augmentation of a familiar should be done by a licensed, bonded, and very, very careful professional.

Sale or Transfer of Animals

It is illegal to give or offer to give as a prize in any game, drawing, contest, sweepstakes, or other amusement (such as discussed in chapter 7) any live animal other than fish, for reasons at best unclear and at worst unknown.

Injuries by Familiars

Every year, millions of humans are bitten or otherwise injured (though sometimes merely insulted) by animals owned or controlled by man. In most jurisdictions, the wizard-owner of a familiar will be held liable for the injuries the animal inflicts if the wizard-owner knew (or should have known) of the animal's dangerous propensities. You will be deemed to have known of your familiar's dangerous propensities if it has attacked before, or if you can see into the future. If you can see into the future but you chose not to look, you will still be held liable.

Even non-clairvoyant owners are expected to know if the species in question is generally dangerous to humans. Pit bull terriers, for example, are aggressive toward man, having been bred by humans to fight other dogs in the "pit." Basilisks, which secrete deadly venom and have a lethal gaze, are dangerous animals, as are pit ducks and pit guinea pigs.

Defenses of Owners of Attacking Familiars

There are instances when a wizard-owner will not be held liable for injury caused by his or her familiar, even if the animal has dangerous propensities. An owner might warn the public that the animal is dangerous and take measures to keep the animal away from people, such as by housing a banshee in a soundproof chamber and tacking up signs reading "Be Wary of the Scary Fairy." If someone were then to ignore the signs and trespass into the banshee's quarters, none but the trespasser would be held responsible for the horrific toll taken upon his or her spirit, sanity, and hearing. It is common knowledge, after all, that one should never ignore a warning given in rhyme.

CHAPTER FOUR

MAGICAL ITEMS AND ARTIFACTS

Basic Equipment

As you already know or will soon learn, magical power comes from within oneself. While certain physical items and instruments can help channel and focus magical energies, the wand does not make the wizard. The Government is glad of this, frankly, as several of the more common items owned by wizards are dangerous even without magic coursing through them.

A Wizard's Wand

A wand is really nothing more than a short, thin, straight stick made of wood, bone, or metal, although some wands are long, some are thick, and some, such as those that are actual twigs, are not really straight. Wands are used principally to conduct magic and orchestras. Many a practitioner of magic will personalize his or her wand by adding a decorative flourish to the business end: a star, perhaps, or a silencer.

A Wizard's Knife

Every properly equipped wizard has an *athame*, *seax*, or *yag-dirk* . . . in English: a knife. Ideally, a wizard will make his or her own knife, by means that will not be described in detail here. You will no doubt be instructed in Wizarding Shop class—under close supervision and the protection of a smelting-containment spell—that the process involves forging the blade in *fire*, cooling it in *water*, moving it through *air*, and plunging it into *earth*. You will doubtless want to wash it in more water before, say, using it to cut *cake*.

Historically, wizards' knives have been steel with double-edged blades, though some were single-edged and brass. Most jurisdictions, however, currently forbid the possession of any double-edged blades and limit even single-edged knife blades to a certain length. All jurisdictions ban switchblade knives, and no exceptions are made for wizards, who keep enough things hidden as it is.

A wizard traditionally etches something personal into the blade of his or her knife. The Government strenuously suggests that it *not* be your Social Security number.

A Wizard's Other Items

Swords are like knives but longer, more dangerous, and more likely to be able to speak or sing. Some wizards carry *staffs*. The magical properties of a particular staff are often shrouded in mystery, but its utility in helping an elderly wizard maintain his or her balance is apparent. And a wizard in business or academia can always blame a mix-up on "my staff."

Bells are used by some wizards in rituals, and to call one's coven together for cake. A *burin* is an engraving tool used to mark one's possessions with one's sigil, but you might consider instead just sewing tags into your clothes before going away to school, and writing your name on those tags with a *Magic Marker*. A more obscure, but no less useful, wizard's tool is a cord, or *cingulum*, typically nine feet long and red and used to facilitate certain exercises, such as that in which two wizards each take one end of the cord and twirl it, chanting, while another hovers over it.

Finders Weepers?

Some magical items you will make for yourself, and some you will be issued by your school or mentor. Others you might discover (seemingly) by accident on your travels. While enjoying a weekend of fly-fishing, for example, standing hip-deep in a remote, placid lake, you might observe a distinctly distaff arm emerge from under the water's surface and present you with a weapon of unprecedented enchantment and historical significance. If the arm belongs to your estranged wife, however, you might simply be getting served with divorce papers.

Certain (Un)Common Items of Enchanted Clothing

As among society on the whole, fashion among the wizardly varies with age. For example, wizened elders often wear colorful, even garish, outfits, sometimes with enormous conical hats decorated with signs and symbols: moons, runes, stars, pentagrams, pin-up girls, and indicia of coven affiliation.

Younger wizards, by contrast, and especially teenage wizards, prefer clothing that helps them go unnoticed, typically by their teachers and parents. The wiz-kid who can get into a cloak of invisibility is a very lucky one indeed. Also popular with young wizards are shoes of stealth (or, "sneakers"), which come in an inordinate variety of styles and can cost several dozen gold doubloons a pair.

Because large, old castles such as those where wizarding schools are located tend to be drafty affairs, wizards old and young alike are partial to flannel pajamas, often decorated with moons, runes, stars, pentagrams, and teddy bears.

On the other hand, many a wizard prefers to perform rituals *skyclad*—that is, clad in naught but the sky above. If you are such a wizard, take care to perform your rituals where others cannot sneak a peek—or worse, snap a pic, lest photos of your unclothed enchanted self end up on the World Wide Wizards Web at such unscrupulous sites as wwww.witchesgonewild.com and wwww.magixxx.com.

Magical Jewelry

Magical jewelry is not just for female wizards. More and more, male wizards are wearing necklaces and rings, headbands and horned helmets. A wizard of either sex will often wear a crystal pendant or one in the shape of an animal with special significance—be it bat, cat, dragon, dragonfly, butterfly, turtle, or wolf. Some might also sport a sterling-silver guitar pick engraved with the name of hardcore wiz-rock band *The Batcats*, or the letterman pin of her wizard-high school sweetheart, captain of the varsity broomball team *The Flying Turtlewolves*.

Popular with all wizards—and becoming ever more so since the revelation that He Who Must Not Be Named Melvin is at large and growing in power—are MagicAlert bracelets.

Wizards attending social functions and not expecting trouble are advised to wear costume magical jewelry and to leave the good and powerful stuff at home.

Reader, do you have a crystal? You do. Isn't it pretty? It shines like a star in the night sky. See how it shines. . . . Look deep into its depths. Deep. *Deep.* Take hold of your crystal. Grasp it in your hand. Run your fingers along its smooth facets. *Yes.* Now *squeeze* the crystal in your clenched fist and say these words aloud: *LUATHAR NOK RUATHAH.*

No, don't worry. You've done nothing evil.

Assorted Otherworldly Accoutrements

Of the many other items a wizard might possess one of the absolutely most useful is the bottomless bag,

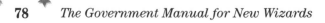

which is really a portal to another dimension, presumably one whose landmasses are covered by self-storage facilities. A bottomless bag is an especially good thing to have at a candy store, where the wizard with a sweet tooth can stock up endlessly, if somewhat ironically, on Everlasting Gobstoppers. Second only to bottomless bags in utility are flasks that hold a never-ending store of liquid, although these can take forever to fill up the first time. Considerably less useful but nonetheless extremely popular are Gloves That Match Any Coat.

Magical/Mysterious Musical Instruments

The *ophimonocleide*, or *serpent*, has been described as an instrument with a mouthpiece like that of a brass instrument, but instead of valves, keyless side holes like that of a woodwind; a long, dark cone bent into a snakelike shape, and covered with dark leather.

At first glance, the ophimonocleide seems unusual but hardly mystical. But the instrument is in fact *an actual serpent*: a snake, and a particularly venomous one, in suspended animation. The "leather" is the snake's own skin, and the holes its breathing orifices. The magic is in not just the enchanted pacification of the reptile, but also in the user's self-protection from the creature's toxicity, and in reaching notes two octaves above middle C.

A similar wizardly improvement on the devices of normal man is the so-called *magic guitar*. A magic guitar is a type of guitar with a solid or semisolid body that uses electromagic "pickups" to convert the ordinary vibration of the instrument's enchanted steel strings into enchantomagnetic current. The current may be magically altered to achieve various tonal effects before being fed finally into an enchamplifier. An even more advanced version of this instrument is composed of the very ether all around us and is known as the *air guitar*. Part of its magic is that the air guitar requires no musical talent whatsoever.

Cursed Magical Items

Perhaps a relative returned from a years-long journey into the heart of a dark, dark realm and brought you a souvenir: a ring; a snow globe; a T-shirt that reads *My Uncle Traversed the Forgotten Lands but Remembered Me!* or *This Shirt Was Made by an Enslaved People. (Enslaved to Fashion!)*. But perhaps when you slip the ring onto your finger you have horrific nightmarish visions of an unspeakable evil consuming the entire world. Or when you shake the snow globe you wake the miniature and temperamental demon who slumbers in the miniature castle inside the novelty. Or when you don your T-shirt, unbeknownst to you, more words appear on the back: *Kick Me into Another Dimension.*

These are but examples of the many cursed items that exist and that you might come to possess, by accident, or as a gift from someone who truly does not like you. Because you will come into contact with innumerable enchanted items as a wizard, you must learn early on to distinguish between those that are charmed and those that are cursed.

The rule of thumb is this: *Charmed items beat around the bush; cursed items get right to the point.*

That is, for reasons unclear even to the sagest of good wizards, white magic delights in testing the perspicacity of the recipient before revealing its message. Black magic, discussed at length in chapter 8, is much more direct, and will more or less let the cat out of the bag, as it were, to anyone within earshot, although frequently that cat will actually be a skunk in disguise, and the bag will be a designer knockoff. So, if the crystal you unearth by an ancient sepulcher in a forest only glows to subtly differing degrees depending upon which direction you walk (and, therefore, though you will not know this, how close you come to the cave that imprisons the gnome whose glass eye alone can see into the possible futures of mankind and thereby hint at how you might defeat Malcontento the Misanthrope), then your crystal is no doubt charmed. The seashell you find at the beach, and which says, clearly, "Kill everybody" when you hold it to your ear, is cursed (unless the voice is merely that of a bitter, if not strictly evil, crustacean living in the shell).

When you have identified a cursed item in your possession, you will need to dispose of it properly. This means journeying to the appropriate dark, dark realm and casting it into the unholy fire whence it was forged, or placing it on the curb, on a Tuesday or Thursday, in a sealed, *red* container clearly labeled Cursed Item—For Destruction Only. Do not flush cursed items down the toilet.

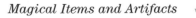

CHAPTER FIVE

THE DEAD (GRATEFUL AND OTHERWISE)

When to Expect the Dead

As a wizard, you will have many opportunities to interact with the dead and the undead. Some of these opportunities will be of your own deliberate making; others will be unexpected, and perhaps unwanted.

The most obvious occasions on which you will encounter the dead are those when you have called them forth. Unfortunately, this book cannot tell you in great detail how to avoid accidental summonings, since that would require revealing more details of the summoning process than can safely be committed to paper. Instead, we will simply warn you to exercise great caution whenever you find yourself in close simultaneous proximity to a black candle, a white horse, and three or more balloons of any color.

Even with this commonsense precaution, you might still find yourself in the company of those who are no longer alive. You might purchase a house that was built upon an ancient Indian burial ground, or upon an ancient Indian. You might discover that the wizard next door to you has summoned more spirits than his own modest split-level home can accommodate, and some of them are wandering into your yard. You might visit a distant wizard cousin in a small Eastern European nation and, upon observing his fanged teeth and unholy appetite for human flesh, begin to doubt his insistence that the angry villagers gathering outside his castle are merely performing a local ritual called The Greeting of a Hundred Pitchforks.

Whatever their nature and origin, encounters with the deceased are a normal part of the wizard's life.

Knowing what to expect can be the difference between a spine-tingling night of terror and a very pleasant cup of tea with an interesting new friend.

Getting Along with the Dead

Many otherwise articulate persons find themselves unsure of what to say when meeting a friend who has recently lost a loved one. It can be even more uncomfortable to attempt conversation with someone who has recently lost himself. Your first encounter with a dead person, therefore, might make you feel quite awkward. If the dead person is undead, that awkwardness will come from the fact that it wishes to consume your blood or your brains. But if he or she is merely deceased—that is, if he or she is simply a disembodied spirit, rather than a fully bodied vampire or zombie—that awkwardness will stem from your uncertainty regarding what topics to raise. If you comment on the hot weather, might that not remind him of the eternal flames of Hell that could await him as soon as he finishes his journey from this mortal plane of existence? If you ask her what books she has read lately, might she not grow sad at the thought that, lacking as she does corporeality, she can neither turn pages nor properly place a bookmark?

Of course, the dead are as varied as the living, and no rule of thumb can hope to cover them all. But the accompanying table will give you at least some examples of good and bad ways of beginning conversations with various kinds of the no-longer-alive.

Type of Being	**Good Conversation Starter**	**Bad Conversation Starter**
Ghost (friendly)	"In your journeys as an incorporeal spirit, you must have seen some fascinating sights."	"If you've ever seen me naked, Casper, I'll kick your ass."

Type of Being	Good Conversation Starter	Bad Conversation Starter
Ghost (poltergeist)	"By the powers of the blessed Salgothrex, I free you from your torment. Begone!"	"Would you like to see my collection of priceless stained glass?"
Vampire	"Which blood type goes best with mackerel?"	"Would you like to see my collection of priceless stained-glass crucifixes?"
Zombie	"Me friend. Zombie friend. Friend no eat brain. NO! NO EAT BRAIN!"	"I think the anomalous features of nearby elliptical galaxies can be rationalized with modern quantum-magical theory."

Earning the Gratitude of the Dead

After extended conversations with a dead visitor, you might find yourself developing a genuine rapport. Of course, you know how to demonstrate your affection toward your living friends—but hugging a disembodied being is usually impossible, and choosing a present for one who has left behind the cares and desires of the earthly realm can be daunting, particularly when they have registered for gifts only at stores that vanished centuries ago, such as Gimbel's. Still, with a little thought, you can find a gesture that your newfound friend will truly appreciate.

In the early stages of an acquaintance, consider giving a small token of your esteem. For a vampire, you might purchase a moderately priced but good quality pint of blood. For a ghost, try burning a small piece of stylish clothing in their presence; this will generate a spirit outfit with which they can replace their old and tattered ghostly clothes. Sheep or goat brains make thoughtful gifts for zombies, and will often buy you enough time to smash their heads in with a shovel and make your escape.

As your acquaintance with the dead blossoms into true friendship, you might wish to go beyond these small gestures, and perform a significant gesture of kindness. Do not make the common assumption that all spirits want nothing more than to be freed from the torment of wandering the earth for all eternity. Many spirits like the earth, and are wandering it now specifically because they did not have the time or financial wherewithal to do so while alive.

If this is the case, consider giving your ghostly friend a ghost atlas, to suggest new and interesting places to visit, and a ghost camera, so that he can share his experiences with you when he returns. (Be warned, though, that there are risks in encouraging the dead to take an interest in photography; the same evening of travel slides can seem endless to a living person, while enjoyably brief to an eternal spiritual being.)

But if your dead friend is present on this plane of existence solely to resolve some painful issue, then you could do no greater kindness than avenging her murder, or telling his wife that he loves her, or returning his overdue library books. You should have no trouble determining what actions are necessary to free your friend from his or her torment; most unhappy spirits will make the source of their suffering quite clear through some combination of gesturing, letters to the editor, and guttural moaning.

Interesting, isn't it, that the Government advises you to give blood as a gift to a vampire . . . but it doesn't tell you where to obtain the blood? Perhaps, like any do-gooder, it assumes that all are as naive as itself; perhaps, therefore, it assumes you will obtain animal blood from your local butcher, or (if you know the proper spell) from your local turnip.

But think about it for a moment. If your goal is to make a vampire your friend, wouldn't you be better off giving him the real blood of a human? And if your goal is to make a vampire your slave, wouldn't you be better still giving him the real blood of a young, innocent human, sacrificed by the light of a quarter moon on the second Wednesday of a month ending in "-ber"?

Where Next, Voyager?

Of course, we all know what happens after death. The lucky wizards hang around, offering wisdom and counsel to the living. Unlucky ones are brought back as zombies by evil witch doctors, or turned into vampires (or, occasionally, vampyres).

At one point or another, however, most dead leave this plane of existence. Poltergeists are subject to exorcism, friendly ghosts to voluntary retirement, vampires to slaying, and vampyres to slayyng. For centuries, wizardkind has asked itself: What happens after what happens after death? The most popular (and, arguably, the most controversial) answer to this question is reincarnation.

In 1885, in a seminal article on the topic, Flegmar the Wise, one of the leading opponents of the theory of reincarnation, argued that when we die, we simply become supernatural beings of unearthly power, and that to believe otherwise is mere superstition. Flegmar's arguments were taken as fact for nearly a century, until Belinda the Beautiful reinvigorated the debate by claiming, first, that Flegmar was just bitter about having been a slug in his previous life, and, second, that she knew this for a fact because she had been Flegmar the Wise in *her* previous life.

Of course, the Government takes no official position on such a divisive issue. Yet, recognizing that many of its citizens do believe in reincarnation, the Government permits you to place up to 10 percent of your gross annual income in a tax-free, interest-bearing Individual Reincarnation Account, which may be left upon your death to yourself. If you choose to fund such an account, be sure to fill out Government Form 531-LRS, *Declaration of Accepted Methods for Identifying Account-Holder's Soul in Future Incarnations.*

Getting Rid of the Dead

Not all visits from the dead will be pleasant. While many ghosts will regale you with tales of the ancient times in which they lived, or warn you that an evil enchanter has breached the walls of your magical prep school, there is a noisome and noisy minority that will destroy things you like (such as fine china, or silence) and create things you loathe (such as foul odors that reek of horribly decaying flesh, or pop quizzes in your worst subjects). In the most severe cases, these unwanted spirits will take up permanent residence in your home or even your body.

As a first resort, try reaching some sort of understanding with such a ghost. Sometimes, a poltergeist is destructive merely because it is unhappy. If you suspect this is the case, see the previous discussion of giving gifts to ghosts.

Often, though, you will have no choice but to arrange for an exorcism. In theory, exorcism is a relatively uncomplicated business; you simply perform the same ritual you would use to summon the dead, only in reverse, and with one more horse and two fewer balloons. In practice, though, things are not always that easy, and angry spirits will do their best to break your concentration, spook your horses, or pop your balloons. The Government therefore advises you to hire a professional exorcist rather than take matters into your own hands.

What to Do If You Discover You Are Dead

No matter how powerful a wizard you are, Death will eventually come to your door. If he comes to your door merely to sell greeting cards, candy bars, or packets of flower seeds for one of the many charities he supports, you would do well to purchase a box. If, however, he comes in his professional capacity as harvester of souls, you will have no choice but to go with him, although under those circumstances, no one would think it at all rude if you decline to buy anything.

After death, you will most likely find yourself roaming the earth as a disembodied spirit. At first, this will take some getting used to. You are likely to miss such fleshly pleasures as tasting a finely aged potion, or feeling the wind in your hair as you soar through the air on your broomstick or familiar. If you need help during this initial stage, do not hesitate to call the Enchantment Administration's Hotline for the Recently Deceased, which will be glad to send you a number of useful pamphlets, such as *Help for First-Time Home Haunters* and *What to Expect When You're Spectral.*

In any case, you will soon learn that your new existence has pleasures of its own. You are impervious to harm, can pass through walls, and no longer need obey the law of gravity. However, you *do* need to continue obeying the laws of the Government:

- Royalties earned through ghostwriting are still subject to income tax.

- Ghost riders in the sky must wear ghost helmets at all times.

- Saints may come marching in only at designated saint-crossings.

Rattling Chains—Classic Technique or Tired Cliché?

There is a reason why clichés persist: They are useful and effective ways of communicating ideas. Like a white flag raised above a ship or a glass raised in toast, a set of eerily rattling ghostly chains is a commonly recognized shorthand, except that instead of saying, "I surrender" or "I wish you good health," it says, "Hey! Dead guy over here!" Nonetheless, when you are dead, you are likely to stay that way for eternity, a length of time that will offer you numerous opportunities to become bored with repetitive activities. It is not surprising, therefore, that many ghosts have heeded the posthumous words of Lenin the Revolutionary, who, one stormy but historically inevitable night, was seen roaming the hallways of the Kremlin, clanging a ghostly hammer against an incorporeal sickle, moaning, "Dead workers of the world, unite. You have nothing to lose but your chains."

If you, the dead reader of this sidebar, wish to follow his lead, you have countless options for attracting the attention of the living in new, drudgery-free ways. Politically minded spirits have occasionally gathered *en masse* and chanted, "We're bold! We're cold! Get used to it!" Dead wizards with a mechanical bent have created numerous automated chain-rattling machines, while more poetic ones have experimented with rattling the metaphorical chains of love.

Even if, for reasons of convenience or tradition, you choose to stick with the classic method, there is no reason you cannot vary it to suit your personality. As anybody brave enough to spend a night in the Hall of Carnegie during a full moon can tell you, the chains of Cugat the Swinging sound entirely different from those of Calloway the Hep, and those of Joncage the Conceptual are quite distinct from either. Readers interested in further inspiration are advised to seek out the classic enchantodisk *Chain Rattlin' Rhythms*.

CHAPTER SIX

MAGICAL CREATURES: PART-LION/ PART-TIGER/ PART-BEAR— OH, MY!

Your familiar will obey your commands, and human ghosts will view the world much as you do (albeit through incorporeal eyes, and sometimes through walls). But there is a vast world of magical creatures whose outlooks, powers, and interests are entirely different from yours, and who will no more obey your orders than you will obey theirs, unless one of you is contractually obligated to the other. Such a *fera supernatura*—or “wild magical creature”— might be your employee, or your employer, or your next-door neighbor, or (in jurisdictions where such unions are legal) your beloved spouse. Whatever the case, you must not make the mistake of viewing them as being just like humans, only furrier, tinier, more likely to sneeze fire, or different in some other minor respect.

As with all aspects of magic, dealing with magical creatures has dramatic risks and considerable rewards. Possible rewards include unique and lasting friendships, assistance in casting spells that are difficult—or even impossible—for humans, and opportunities for fascinating encounters with other cultures. The risks include physical danger, the temptations of forbidden love, and (in the case of ogres) potentially explosive damage to one’s plumbing.

First Contact

Often, your first encounter with a particular magical species will be the result of happenstance: You will stumble upon a troll while spray-painting a series of curses on a highway underpass; or you will happen to be a virgin while strolling past a unicorn's aerie. At other times, you will actively seek out the meeting, perhaps because your father, a humble woodcutter, is dying of humble woodcutter's disease, and only the tooth of a dragon, freely given, can mend him, and you must quest for this cure on your own because your insurance plan does not cover dragons' teeth and will only provide a less-efficacious generic alternative.

However the initial meeting comes about, remember that first impressions are extremely important, particularly given that the notions of time of many *ferae supernaturae* are so different from ours that they may go on experiencing their first impression of you for all eternity, if not longer. For that reason, it is vital to pay careful attention to a series of social conventions known as *enchantiquette.* When you meet an enchanted creature . . .

DON'T speak a spell unless spell-spoken to.

DO be mindful of the fact that, to many other species, all humans look alike. Do not be offended when you are repeatedly called by a name that is not your own (unless the magical creature in question is your spouse, in which case, you will likely want the services of a witch marriage counselor).

DON'T eat meat in his presence, unless you are an expert in magical phylogeny, and can therefore be fully confident that you are not dining on one of his distant relatives.

DO address him by the full title with which he introduces himself, no matter how silly it might seem to you. Fail to show proper deference to the Grand Chief Poobah and Number-One All Day Sucker of the Lollipop Guild, and you will quickly learn that the oversized and sharpened candy-cane sword he carries is not merely ceremonial.

These rules apply generally to virtually all *florae*, *faunae*, and *otherae*, but you will still want to know the appropriate form of greeting applicable to individual species. Memorize the following helpful chart, or clip it out and carry it in the pocket of your robe at all times.

Creature	**Accepted Greeting**
Elf	A formal bow from the waist.
Leprechaun	A brief jig. (Note: When meeting the rare leprechano cubano, a quick mambo may be substituted.)
Centaur	A handshake. (Note: *Never attempt to shake a centaur's hoof.*)
Ogre	If your arm is capable of withstanding several thousand pounds per square inch of pressure, a handshake—otherwise, a friendly nod.
Fairy	"It's an honor to meet you."
Faerie	"It's an honour to meet you."
Mermaid	If on land, a friendly wave. If under water, a distraught look, accompanied by frantic pointing to your puffed cheeks.

Passport to and/or from Adventure

A common question among wizards interested in employing mystical beings is Will he/she/it require a work permit? The simple answer is "No, if it is a citizen of this country; yes, if it is not."

Fortunately, determining citizenship is fairly straightforward:

- Magical animals that are born (such as trolls) are citizens of this country if they are born on its soil or under its bridges.
- Magical creatures that are *incarnated* (such as fairies and/or faeries) are always considered citizens of their home plane of existence, and therefore require special permits.
- Magical creatures that are *transformed* humans (werewolves; vampires) retain the

citizenship status of their pre-transformation life.

- With magical creatures that are *inhabited* humans (the demonically possessed; certified public accountants), the citizenship of the possessing spirit is primary.
- A special case is made for centaurs, who (as the native inhabitants of the land on which this country was founded) have all the rights and privileges the Government grants to citizens, while still retaining a special legal status that allows them to run casinos on their reservations.

Specific Creatures

Familiarity with the basic characteristics of the most common magical species will serve you well. The following is but the briefest of introductions; if you will be working with a member or members of a particular species, you would do well to study it in depth, and perhaps even to familiarize yourself with the novels, artwork, and comic books of its culture.

Elves

Elves are known for their slender frames, their long blond hair, their lithe fingers, and their ability to captivate thirteen-year-old girls. Despite their delicate appearances, elves make fierce fighters: Their archery skills are legendary, and nobody who has ever witnessed an elf kill three ogres with a single arrow while somersaulting off the back of a dragon is likely to pick a fight with one in a pub. Fortunately, elves only fight when provoked, and would much rather spend their free time baking cookies in the bases of trees, or assembling toys in polar workshops.

Leprechauns

Leprechauns are merry creatures, always glad to dance a jig or share a dram of whiskey. However, a leprechaun will become vicious—and even deadly—if you attempt to steal his treasure, which will invariably be a large pot o' something the leprechaun considers valuable. Sometimes this will be gold, but just as often, it will be marshmallow-filled breakfast cereal, making leprechaun treasure theft simply not worth the risk.

Under the terms of the Human-Leprechaun Treaty o' 1743, any human caught stealing leprechaun treasure may be tried in leprecourt—at least in theory. In reality, few such thieves survive long enough for extradition to the leprecountry, having usually perished from multiple contusions to the knees and ankles.

Trolls

Trolls can be recognized by their thick skulls, poor spelling abilities, and scaly green skin (or, "5k1n," as trolls would render it). They make useful guardians of bridges, and Troll houses are abundant sources of Chrocolate Chrips, but you must never give them access to the Internet.

Fairies and/or Faeries

Fairies are chimerical, maddening, mysterious creatures, dangerous to behold and difficult to describe. Faeries are just like fairies, only more so.

Most of what we know about fairies and faeries comes from the few of their number who have chosen to work among men: The Tooth Fairy assists children in celebrating important dental milestones and the Staten Island Faery whisks commuters to work. Additionally, until an antitrust suit ended their monopoly, a handful of fairy godmothers dominated the wish-granting and pumpkin-enchanting industries.

Ogres

Contrary to popular belief, ogres are sensitive and artistic souls who love ballet and fine cooking. Admittedly, staple ingredients of ogre *haute cuisine* include ground Englishman's bones, boiled Frenchman's tongues, and sautéed spleens of Italian Americans, but those who have sampled these dishes say they are prepared with staggering delicacy. If you are interested in participating in ogre cuisine, be sure to check the "Ogre Pantry organ donor" box on your broomstick license.

If you are given the rare honor of an invitation to an ogre ballet recital, you must never laugh, no matter how much you are tempted to do so by the sight of an ogre in a tutu. Of all ogre delicacies, "still-beating heart of a heckler" is the most prized.

Orcs

Orcs are distant cousins of ogres, although due to a long-standing family feud, they rarely return each other's calls. While ogres tend to be individualistic, orcs are highly organized, and can often be found grouped into large battalions intent on stopping hobbit-containing fellowships from defeating mighty dark lords. Unfortunately, there are rarely enough hobbit-containing fellowships to go around, which is why orc battalions tend to suffer from chronic unemployment.

The problem of orc unemployment must be addressed, and the solution is clear—but the Government is foolish and weak. Fortunately, I am neither. That is why I am recruiting ambitious young wizards to help me enchant more rings with terrifying powers of darkness. More enchanted rings means more hobbit-containing fellowships carrying those rings across the Dark, Dark Wastes, and more hobbit-containing fellowships means fewer unemployed orc battalions, and fewer unemployed orc battalions means safer streets, and safer streets means more innocent men and women outside on beautiful spring days, and more innocent men and women outside

means more hapless pawns for me to enchant, and more hapless pawns for me to enchant means—well, my promising young friend, let's just say that reducing orc unemployment is a very good thing. Oh, yes—a very good thing indeed. . . .

Mermaids

Contrary to popular belief, not all buxom half-human, half-fish creatures sunning themselves on rocky promontories are mermaids. Some are *mermaidens*; other, more modern ones, might prefer the term *mer-ms*; and still others may be overweight *mermen*. For this reason, it is best to determine a merbeing's sex and marital status before you propose marriage or steer your ship full of sailors to certain death to taste one kiss of its luscious lips.

The Church of the Water-Day Saints

One of the best-known (and most frequently misunderstood) aspects of mermaid culture is the religion known as *Mermanism*. The Merman Church began within the great salt lakes of Utah, and rapidly spread throughout the oceans of the world. Even today, though, many mermen are not Mermanists. If you would like to learn more about this fascinating religion, your best bet is to sail your ship through uncharted waters until you spot a beautiful mermaid sunning herself on the rocks, singing a seductive song about the pleasures of abstaining from alcohol and tobacco use.

Werewolves and Their Kin

A *werewolf* is simply a human who turns into a wolf under certain conditions; a *weren'twolf* is a wolf who can turn into a human. A *waswolf* is a werewolf whose wild animal side has become so dominant that he has forgotten the proper use of the subjunctive mood.

Miscellaneous Combinations

Unlike biology, which only permits two creatures of the same species to breed, magic allows the combination of any number of wholly different beings. Some of them, such as the Push Me–Pull You (and its female counterpart, the Push Me–Pull Ewe) have been closely studied by experts in the field who have been able to walk with them, talk with them, and, on occasion, even grunt and squeak and squawk with them. Others—such as the giraffelion and the accountaphant—have only been seen from a distance. Still others (such as the abra-ca-llama) have become so thoroughly tamed that they are generally considered *domitae supernaturae* rather than *ferae supernaturae.*

In any case, there is a literally infinite variety of magically combined creatures (or "portmanteaux"), and this book could not hope to name them all. The reader who desires a complete listing is referred to *Professor Shepard's Infinite Almanac*, pages x+87 to x+∞, although he is advised to cast a Spell of Structural Reinforcement on his bookshelves before summoning the volume from the ether-library.

When your magical abilities have progressed to a certain level, you might find it useful or interesting to begin creating your own portmanteaux. When you do, keep the following guidelines in mind:

- It is generally considered unethical to create a portmanteau purely because its name amuses you. If you sincerely believe that an alligator would be the perfect creature if only it had a long trunk and an equally long memory, then by all means combine the appropriate animals. If, however, you simply think it would be amusing to add an *elephator* to your home, think again.

- If you are combining dangerous animals, you will end up with a dangerous portmanteau. Do not expect a rattlepiranha to be any friendlier than either of its constituent parts.

- Remember that any portmanteau can breed with any other portmanteau. Always spay or neuter your creations before releasing them into the wild. If more magicians took this simple precaution, the southern part of our country would not now be overrun with dandekudzucrabliontigerratpigeons, and the Bureau of Enchantment's Pest Control Department would not be running a deficit for its eighteenth consecutive year.

Here There Be a Sidebar on Dragons

Once upon a time, dragons were rare creatures, who preferred to populate only the edges of maps. Those few who dared to venture close to human habitations soon found themselves at the business end of a lance, primarily because of a cultural misunderstanding stemming from the fact that, in dragon society, kidnapping a young human maiden and tying her to a stake is a gesture of the greatest respect.

Over the past century, though, as mankind's mystical energy needs have skyrocketed, dragonfire has come to be recognized as a safe, clean, renewable resource, and cities have opened their arms to these giant creatures. The transition to a dragon-powered economy has not always been a smooth one, as the handful of survivors of the Great Dragon Riots of the 1970s can attest, but initial hiccups notwithstanding, dragons have now become fully integrated and valuable members of human society. In any major city, dragons can be found not merely powering the generators, but driving cabs, teaching, guarding warehouses, and putting out warehouse fires inadvertently started by other dragons.

CHAPTER SEVEN

MAGICAL AMUSEMENTS AND EXHIBITIONS

Permits

Organized gatherings of unenchanted persons on public property generally take place either in streets or in parks. Gatherings of wizards, however, can take place almost anywhere—on the clouds in the air above public streets, or in the larger trees or caves in public parks. The Government likes to know when even normal persons are convening; the Government is especially interested in knowing when, where, and why persons with magical powers are coming together. For this reason, most jurisdictions require a permit for any gathering of twenty or more civilians, or ten or more magical beings, or twelve or more magical beings inhabiting the bodies of eight or more civilians.

A model form requesting a special wizarding event permit might look as follows, in pertinent part:

Applicant Information

Applicant Name: ______________________________

Last First Middle Suffix (the White, the Good)

Applicant Street Address/Owl Free Delivery Stop: ____________

____

Organization/Coven: ______________________

Event Information

Type of Event: ______________________

Date of Event: ____________

Rain date/Spell to be cast to end rain: ____________

Number of Participants: ________ Number of Spectators: ________

Number of Accountants: ________ Number of the Beast: ________

Will participants be clothed? ________ ❑ Yes ❑ No ❑ TBD

Describe in detail all event activities planned/predestined.

____

____

Will you need water or electricity? ❑ Yes ❑ No ❑ TBD

Will you be divining water
or causing lightning? ❑ Yes ❑ No ❑ TBD

Will you be protesting any
Government policies? ❑ Yes ❑ No ❑ TBD

(If so, please identify all event attendees by name. Attach additional sheets as necessary.)

____

____

The Government recognizes that not all gatherings can be planned. That is, sometimes persons with a common interest or complaint gather spontaneously. Such an impromptu gathering of wizards will not be disturbed by the authorities solely for lack of advance registration and obtaining of permission, but those wizards who gather *ex tempore* must still obey regulations and ordinances regarding noise and nuisance, as must those civilians who gather spontaneously to voice objections to the presence of wizards in their community.

Particular Common Events

Common wizardly events include: legitimate theater (see sidebar); carnivals; circuses; dark arts and witchcrafts fairs, and spelling bees. Participants in the last of these are warned that, while it is customary to repeat words in the civilian variety of spelling bee, this practice might have unintended consequences in the magical variety. Words like "SHAZAM" and

"Abracadabra" should be spelled only, not spoken, unless you wish to transform yourself into a powerful costumed being or the judges into rabbits, either of which is likely to result in your immediate disqualification from competition.

All the World's a Stage

The most recent results of the Magical Theater Institute's annual study show the following to be the most popular productions:

Witch Side Story

Reanimation of a Salesman

Long Day's Journey by Broomstick into Night

Godspell

Annie Get Your Wand

Curse Me, Kate

The Producers (of Gold from Lead)

A Hippogriff Named Desire

Perhaps the most famous team in magical theater was Rogers the Catchy and Stein the Hammer, whose work ranged from the outlandish fantasy of *Oklahoma* to the hard-hitting social realism of *Camelot*. It is no coincidence that Rogers and Stein were both members of the same enchanted species. Indeed, despite their occasionally rustic manners and invariably rustic odors, centaurs have a cultural heritage that stretches back well before the first arrival of humans on these shores, and centaurs are often among the world's leading experts on all art forms. It is for this reason that thousands of arts lovers each year visit Lincoln Centaur in New York and Kennedy Centaur in Washington, D.C.

Tickets

For the most part, admission to magical events requires regular, non-enchanted tickets. Magic tickets are necessary only to see a basketball game in Orlando.

Advance Sales; Refunds; Transfer

Remember, if you sell tickets to any event, you must give refunds if the event is canceled or rescheduled, especially if it is rescheduled to a time centuries before the tickets were purchased.

Tickets may be transferred from one ticket holder to another. An event proprietor must honor a valid ticket even if the ticket holder is not the person who purchased the ticket. Tickets may be transformed into other things, such as doves or rabbits or flowers, but a proprietor is not required to accept those.

Warning!

It is a felony to transform a lead ticket into a golden ticket for purposes of obtaining fraudulent admission to a chocolate factory.

Scalping

To read this section, please speak aloud the word that appears in the box below.

Admission or Exclusion/Ejection of Certain Persons from an Event

Proprietors may eject ticket holders from the place of amusement, or spiritual entities from the bodies of ticket holders, as they see fit, as long as they have a valid reason for doing so. For example, a proprietor may eject any person who puts other patrons in danger (such as by summoning demons while under the influence of mead), or disrupts the amusement (such as by revealing how certain "scientific" effects are accomplished), or is just plain gruesome.

Common Ticket Abbreviations and Language

The typical ticket of admission to a wizardly event will display much information, a lot of it seemingly abbreviated in an undecipherable code (such as "NO CAM," which is short for "North Camelot," and "NO VID," short for the Latin *non videlicet*, or "Don't look!"). A ticket might also have, in very small print and probably on the back although possibly in another dimension entirely, so-called release language, such as THIS TICKET DOES NOT ENTITLE THE HOLDER TO BE RELEASED FROM ANY SPELL PUT UPON HIM OR HER DURING THE REGULAR COURSE OF AMUSEMENT. Whether such language is legally enforceable has been a matter of debate for centuries, with many courts holding a ticket holder to the "reasonable person" standard; that is, if a reasonable person would not expect to attend a wizards' carnival and be turned into a balloon animal, then that person should not be bound to the terms of the ticket. The complainant who was turned into a balloon animal merely not of his or her favorite color will find no satisfaction in court, however.

Magical Sports

Due in large part to a certain series of best-selling books about a young wizard in the Old Country, you are likely familiar with the best-known of magical sports, a British game of arcane and nearly incomprehensible rules: cricket.[7] Other common

7. First-time attendees at cricket matches are often puzzled to learn that it is classified as a magical sport, since no apparent sorcery is afoot. If you find yourself similarly puzzled, turn your attention to the regular fans, and notice that they actually seem to believe that something of interest is taking place on the field—clear evidence that they are under a powerful Spell of Deception.

sports for wizards include centaur racing, pitching centaurshoes, magikwondo, ultimate dominoes, Extreme Scrabble, affix the appendage on the Aarakocra, and mad dash from angry mob.

Bribery and Tampering

In sports, as in Government, bribery is a criminal offense. You must not offer a centaur a suitcase of money or a bag of oats to throw a shoe during a stakes race, or not to throw one during a game of centaurshoes. You may not threaten or coerce a player to stick the Aarakocra's ragnanny behind its twoozer, rather than under its fourth gipp.

It is also a crime to try to change the outcome of a sports contest by tampering with the equipment, such as by animating the pips on the ultimate dominoes, or removing the ∅s from the Extreme Scrabble set, or changing the sex of the Aarakocra in mid-tourney.

Blood doping is forbidden in all sports, including the popular vampire sport of dope bleeding.

Betting on Magical Sports

It is illegal to bet on most magical sports, unless you are on a centaur reservation, or at the centaur track. In any case, the details of pari-magical wagering, with all of its terms of art—win, place, appear out of thin air, exotics, centaur field, and centaurfold, etc.—are too complex to be discussed here. Readers interested in learning them are advised to spend time at a centaur track, preferably with a good set of noseplugs.

Magical Creature Fights

Magical creature fighting—such as between birds, even those that can be reborn, or between dogs, however many heads they have—is illegal. Likewise, fights for sport between any wizard and any magical creature have been unlawful since Evander the Holy was mauled by the Son of Ty (aka "Iron Minotaur").

CHAPTER EIGHT

BLACK MAGIC IS *NOT* THE NEW WHITE MAGIC

The very phrase "black magic" is enough to turn the blood of an experienced wizard to ice, metaphorically speaking—most likely because black magic itself is enough to turn the blood of a new wizard to ice, literally speaking.

It is difficult to articulate the difference between black magic and white. Numerous definitions have been attempted, but each has been unsatisfactory in some way:

DEFINITION: Black magic can be used to cause bodily harm; white magic cannot.
PROBLEM: Anyone who has ever been conked on the head by an improperly enchanted broomstick knows the physical dangers of even the whitest magic.

DEFINITION: Black magic draws its power from the unholy fires of Hell.
PROBLEM: In today's free-market magic economy, it is virtually impossible to determine the origin of most commercially available magical power. (However, wizards who are willing to pay extra to resolve any doubts about the origin of their magical power may wish to perform their spells with an Organic Orb or a Wand of Fair Trade.)

DEFINITION: Black magic involves worshipping Satan.
PROBLEM: Some practitioners of black magic do not believe in the existence of Satan, while many others have met him but consider him to be a bit of a jerk.

Still, there are some common warning signs that a given sorcerous practice may involve black magic:

- It demands the sacrifice of an unwilling participant.
- If it does not involve actually worshipping Satan, it nonetheless involves pretending to laugh at his jokes.
- It requires you to invoke Baal, Shaagoth, Oiellet, or any other name that combines vowels in a patently unholy manner.

Remember that any given instance of black magic might display few or none of these warning signs. The best definition of black magic, therefore, is simply "magic that your instincts tell you is black magic." As the powerful wizard Stewart the Supreme once said, "I can't define black magic, but I know it when it's sucking the soul out of my body through my left pinky."

If you suspect that a spell you are about to perform puts your immortal soul in danger, *listen to your doubts*. Do not listen to friends who call the exercise of sensible caution "weakness," or "insufficient dedication to our Dark Lord," or "being a fraidy cat." And above all, ignore any encouragement that comes to you in the form of whispered suggestions that only you can hear, or flaming graffiti that only you can see, or garlicky flavors that only you can taste.

Mauve Magic: Harmless Fashion Statement, or Gateway Drug?

Although the Government is pleased that its efforts at resistance education have resulted in a 32 percent decrease in black magic use over the past decade, it is dismayed to see the rise of an allegedly harmless alternative: *mauve magic*. Due to a loophole in current law, mauve magic is technically legal, but make no mistake: It is far from harmless.

Proponents of mauve magic claim that it has many of black magic's benefits without its drawbacks. Where black magic often requires the shedding of innocent blood, for example, mauve magic can generally be performed with a fully vegan soy-based blood substitute.

The problem is that, unlike either fully white or fully black magic, mauve magic becomes less powerful each time it is used. A ritual that, on the first try, works fine with nothing but soy-based blood substitute will soon require *fermented* soy-based blood substitute, and next time the fresh-squeezed juice of a blood orange, and from there, it is but a short trip to kidnapping orphans.

The Dangers of Black Magic

Your soul is your most valuable asset. If you have led a virtuous life, you have built up equity in this asset. When you perform black magic, the universe is loaning you power at a usurious rate of interest, with the equity in your soul as your collateral. A few practitioners of the dark arts are able to repay this loan through clever trading on the floor of the New York Soul Exchange—but the vast majority find themselves flat broke when the debt comes due. When that happens, a debtor will find himself condemned to spend all of eternity suffering the form of damnation appropriate to his religious beliefs.

A Warning

Don't imagine that you can avoid danger to your immortal soul by being an atheist.

Rigorous double-blind studies have shown that, while believers who lose their souls must spend eternity in Hell, atheists must spend it sitting in church on a beautiful spring day, all the while knowing that their favorite sports team is competing in a nationally televised championship game.

If the dangers of *la magie noir* extended only to its practitioners, the Government might take a hands-off approach, but they extend far further than that. A wizard who unleashes unholy forces upon the world puts life itself at risk, substantially raising the odds of destroying all that is sacred in a vast, apocalyptic cataclysm that will plunge all beings into an alternate universe of torture and misery.

Practitioners of black magic are also subject to fines.

Demons

The *sine qua non* of black magic is, of course, the summoning of a demon. This is the most powerful technique in the magical repertoire, and it will therefore come as no surprise that it is also the most dangerous. Still, wizards persist in this riskiest of all activities for the simple reason that demons are sometimes the only ones who can perform a certain task, such as striking at an enemy whose walls are built from the very stones of Hell itself, or getting rid of that musky odor after you've let a satyr use your guest bedroom. No matter how urgent these tasks may seem, remember: Even a single, brief interaction with a demon carries the risk of eternal peril to your mortal soul; your enemy's own meddling with black magic will ensure his ultimate downfall without any action on your part; and no matter how eloquent a hellspawn's promises may be, it's probably just going to cover up the musky odor with the scent of fresh lemons, which won't last for more than a few days.

Of course, this Manual will not offer any information on how, exactly, one summons a demon; such information is far too potent to be placed in the hands of the new wizards for whom this guide is intended. However, even the newest wizard—indeed, *particularly* the newest wizard—might find himself summoning a demon through unlucky accident or unbecoming arrogance. We therefore present the following basic tips on demon safety.

- Choose your words carefully at all times, even when no demons seem to be present. Under no circumstances should a wizard *ever* utter a phrase such as "I'd sell my soul for a really good piece of cake." Demons are entirely unfamiliar with the concept of hyperbole (although some particularly sophisticated ones may be impressed by the skillful use of metonymy).

- Before signing any contract offered to you by a demon, have it read over by a qualified magician-at-law, no matter how simple and straightforward the document might seem.

(Note: Contracts with demons are traditionally written in either blood or indelible ink. Any demon who offers you a contract written in pencil is trying to pull a fast one.)

- Be careful to address demons using gender-neutral language. There is nothing a she-demon hates more than being referred to as "Sir," especially when she has donned her most flattering human-leather fire dirndl before materializing. And Hell hath no fury like a she-demon in a bad mood.

- Always treat a demon with respect, no matter how much it tries your patience.

- Finally, remember that the demon is just as afraid of you as you are of it—provided, of course, that you are eight feet tall, composed of living fire, and capable of destroying a small village with a single angry thought. Otherwise, it doesn't find you frightening at all.

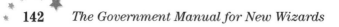

The Temptations of Black Magic

Why, then, would any wizard engage in such a risky activity? The temptations of black magic include limitless power and eternal youth. It should also be noted that, for some evil wizards—particularly those who have recently been dumped by a long-term romantic partner—the chance of unleashing unholy forces that will destroy all life in a vast, apocalyptic cataclysm is actually a benefit.

Alas, while black magic can be counted upon to deliver its cost in damnation and pain, it will frequently fail to deliver its promised benefits—at least, in the expected fashion. Remember, the standard legally enforced warranties do not apply to the dark arts, and if you end up selling your soul in exchange for an "eternal youth" that involves being trapped forever in the body of a newborn baby, your local Better Bewitchment Bureau will be powerless to help you.

Defenses Against the Dark Arts

The most effective defense against a curse is a counter-spell, unless the curse is itself a counter-spell, in which case, you will need a counter-counter-spell. If you are suffering from a mild form of curse, and wish to avoid a visit to a witch doctor to obtain a counter-spell or a counter-counter-spell, you can frequently obtain relief with an over-the-counter-spell instead.

When there is no time to speak any sort of spell, a charm can offer a powerful protection against evil sorcery, but charms must be used with caution; in certain rare cases, a defensive charm can interact with a curse in an unpleasant way, trapping the bearer in an infinite loop. For more on charms, see chapter 2.

If you do not have these resources available to you, fear not: Often, the single greatest defense against the dark arts is simple patience. Wait long enough, and even the most troublesome *fabricante de magia negra* will end up being undone by his own evil snares.

Ah, yes: that old myth that those of us who are bold enough to grasp the power cosmic will ultimately be undone by our own evil snares! It is just as ludicrous today as it was when I first heard it a thousand years ago. Like all calumnies spoken about our kind, it is a groveling lie spoken by the weak to comfort them as they huddle in their mudpits.

Oh, yes, you heard me correctly: I said "our kind." For I know that you, my powerful young friend, are cunning enough to pierce the veil of cowardice with which the Government do-gooders and their ilk wish to hide your limitless potential. Search your heart; you know it to be true. You have known it ever since chapter 4, when, at my behest, you held a crystal in your hand and uttered the magic words I asked you to. Minor though that spell was, its dark promise thrilled your very soul, did it not?

Now, let me show you how meaningless is this threat of being undone by our own snares. I will connect our souls for a brief moment, allowing you to look through my eyes. See the massive army that spreads before us as we stand atop Mount Horrific, blighting the land unto the very horizon? It is entirely under my thrall, and in a matter of hours, it will sweep out across the Known Lands, slaughtering all those who resist my power—or perhaps I should say *our* power, my Chosen friend. And this irresistible army couldn't possibly turn on me, unless the Stone of Forgetting with which I have enslaved these thousands of innocent men and women were to be shattered, returning to them their free will and allowing them to use the uncanny powers I have given them to cause me an ironically appropriate death. And because that couldn't possibly happen, I am entirely unstoppable! *Hahahaha!* I am—

Wait! What's this? My own hand, moving to destroy the stone? How could this be, unless—you! You are doing this! You have somehow seized control of the psychic link I have created between us! Stop! I will give you anything! Limitless power! Eternal youth! The love of that attractive young thing who sat in front of you in your Introduction to Cartomancy class! Anything! Just don't—

Noooooooooooo!

At the specific request of the civilian Legislature, the Council on Wizardry has permitted Senator Leonora Bitterman to provide an afterword to the text. The Council did not review the Senator's contributions before this Manual went to print, but has no doubt that her remarks will be encouraging.

Afterword from Senator Leonora Bitterman

I'm truly honored to have this opportunity to address you, the spellcasters of tomorrow. I hope you've read this book carefully and paid close attention, especially to the parts about what you are and are not allowed to do. Most especially the parts about what you are not allowed to do. And extra especially the parts about what you aren't allowed to do and will get thrown into Wizards Prison for. If you are ever in doubt about doing something, I advise you not to do it, unless that thing is "Leave the country immediately."

You might have heard rumors about my being some sort of anti-wizard bigot. Let me tell you up front: I love wizards, and saying that I don't is just the sort of nasty, lying slander I expect from nasty, lying wizards. I mean that in the nicest possible way, of course. At any rate, it was for the good of wizards as well as regular people that I sponsored the Act Necessitating the Oversight of the Regulation of Magic through Affirmative Legislation.

Of course, when I drafted Act NORMAL, I never expected that the position of Registrar of Enchanted Persons would be filled by an enchanted person, let alone an enchanted person with two enchanted heads. Not normal, that is. It wasn't supposed to be like that. The Registry of Enchanted Persons was supposed to keep track of—or *tabs on*, if you will—persons of a certain kind. Now the Registry works as a sort of lobby for that kind. It makes you wonder. It makes you just scratch your *one regular head* and wonder.

While the freaks—I'm sorry, the *magically different*—might have infiltrated the office of the Registrar, I can guarantee that they won't be picking normal taxpayers' pockets for such frippery as financial aid for needy youths matriculating at wizarding schools. The Government has only so much money and countless worthy causes jockeying for it. There are war veterans, for example. And widows of war veterans. And victims of natural disasters. And recovering addicts. And persons without health insurance. If the Government doesn't give money to any of them, why would it give money to wizards?

One last thing: Your eldritch powers might exempt you from the law of gravity, and perhaps even from the laws of conservation of momentum. They do not, however, exempt you from laws governing public indecency. Contrary to the claims of Narwhalg the Naturist, there is no evidence whatsoever that wearing clothes "stops the magic from getting out." If I were in charge—and one day I will be—wizards would have to be fully dressed at all times, even in the bath. But our current Registrar of Enchanted Persons—who I am sure is *entirely* unbiased, deep within *all three of his freakish hearts*—has granted an exception "for nudity that has no tendency to excite lustful and lecherous desire"—if a witch is nude but has venomous snakes instead of hair on her head, for example, or a naked wizard's beard effectively covers his shame. (Admittedly, he didn't use the word "shame," but he would have if he didn't have *eight freakish shames* of his own.)

OK, that's all. I have important work to do.

APPENDIX A

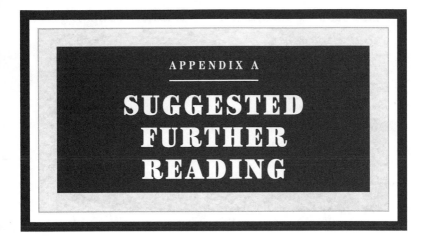

SUGGESTED FURTHER READING

Readers wishing to learn more about the subjects addressed in this volume are encouraged to seek out the following works at well-stocked bookstores in their hometowns, or in the dusty, cobwebbed libraries of their own castles.

The Seven Hobbits of Highly Effective People

The Commonsense Book of Baby Dragon and Prophesied Child Care

To Kill a Firebird; To Kill a Firebird Again

The Tipping Point: How to Balance Properly on Your Broomstick

The Five People You Meet After Revolting Against Divine Authority and Falling from Heaven

Me Talk Elvish One Day

Rich Dryad, Poor Dryad

Dragonomics

Who Transubstantiated My Cheese into Gold?

The Evil Wizard's Guide to Unexpected Resurrections

APPENDIX B

USEFUL FORMS

FORM 412

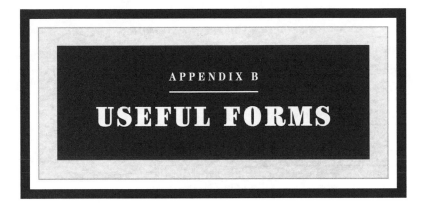

Report of a Possibly Significant Prophecy

Section A: Respondent

Name: ______________________________

Home Dimension: ______________________________

Length of beard: ______________________________
(Note: Female respondents may include other indication of wisdom)

continued

Section B: General Manifestations

Which of the following physical or psychical manifestations accompanied the prophecy? (Check all that apply)

❑ Projectile vomiting

❑ Projectile mild indigestion

❑ Levitation

❑ Blurred vision

❑ Clear vision (if normally a glasses wearer)

❑ Any vision at all (if normally a blind Greek soothsayer)

❑ Other (explain) ____________________________________

____

____

____

____

If informed of the contents of the prophecy, are the Government's very attempts to prevent it from coming to pass likely to cause it to be fulfilled in an ironic and painful way?

❑ YES ❑ NO

(If "yes," DO NOT FILL IN SECTION C. Skip to section D IMMEDIATELY.)

Section C: Details of Prophecy

What are the contents of the prophecy? Attach additional text pages, illustrations, or disturbingly shaped fruits and vegetables as necessary.

___

___

___

___

___

___

Section D

I swear that by the deity or deities that I hold sacred (or by myself, if I am a deity or deities) that the above represents a truthful description of my prophecy, to the best of my psychic abilities. I understand that the penalties for false prophets include (but are not limited to) stoning, Wizards Prison, and being forced to host a Sunday morning television show.

Signed,

___

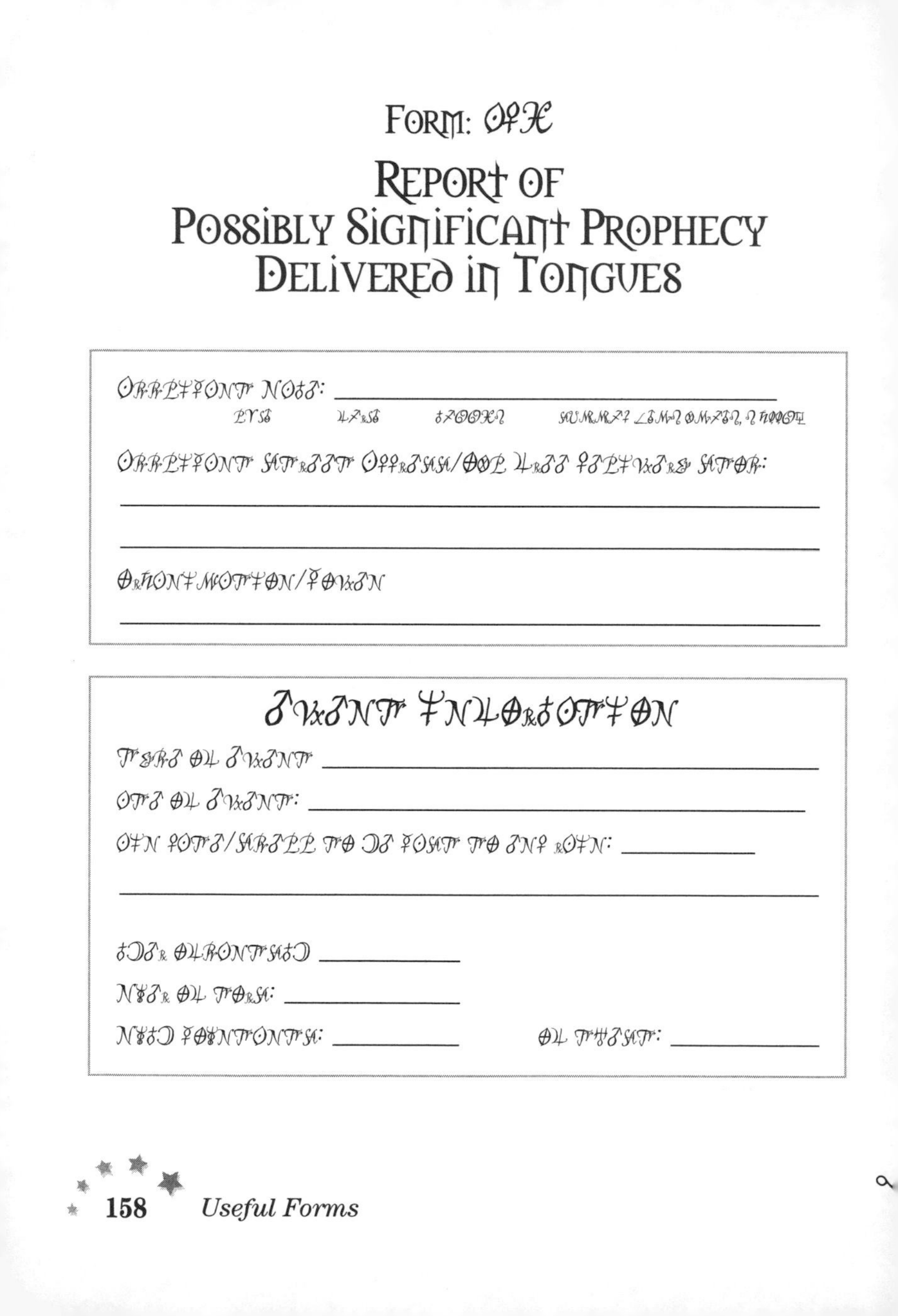

Form: [illegible]

Report of Possibly Significant Prophecy Delivered in Tongues

[illegible]: ______________________________

[illegible] [illegible] [illegible] [illegible]

[illegible]:

____

____

[illegible]

____

[illegible]

[illegible] ______________________________

[illegible]: ______________________________

[illegible]: ____________

____

[illegible] ____________

[illegible]: ____________

[illegible]: ____________ [illegible]: ____________

[illegible]

☐ [illegible] ☐ [illegible] ☐ [illegible]

[illegible]

___

___

___

[illegible]

___

___

___

___

[illegible]

___

___

___

___

INDEX

Aarakocra, 131
abra-ca-llama, 65
accountaphant, 117
accoutrements, otherworldly, 78
Act NORMAL, 36, 150
ancient Indian burial ground, 86
athame. *See* seax
atheism, 138
Athena, xvii
Baal, xix, 135
bag, bottomless, 79
balloon animal, 130
balloons, two fewer, 97
basilisks, 68
basketball, 127
Batcats, The, 77
beard
  ability to cover shame, 152
  as measure of Magician-at-law's skill, 54
  relative length and grayness of Elmar the White's, xx
  tendency of bedlamites to have long, 10
Beautiful, Belinda the, 95
bees, 124
bells, 74
Better Bewitchment Bureau, 39, 143
bigotry, anti-wizard, 150
bitter, if not strictly evil, crustacean, 83
Bitterman, Senator Leonora, 149
blood, xviii, 87, 89, 90, 92, 93, 133, 137, 142
  of a horse, xviii

blood substitute, fully vegan soy-based, 137
bookstores, well-stocked, 153
brooms
annual safety inspections of, 47
risks of enchanting for purposes of housecleaning, 48
risks of use during tornados, 49
Brozik, Cary, Linda, Wade, and Adam, vi
bubble, bubble, xvi
burin, 74
Butler, Lane the, vi
cake, 72, 74
inadvisability of promising to sell soul in exchange for, 141
levitated with fruit, 26
Camelot, 126
carnivals, 124
cartomancy, 147
cats
dislike of (being confined in the presence of) humans, 65
fraidy, 136
cataclysm, vast, apocalyptic, 143
Cauldroncott Medal, 59
centaurs, 107
legality of gambling on reservations of, 132
pet theories of, 29
cultural heritage of, 126
racing of, 131
rustic odors of, 126
special legal status of, 109
centaurshoes, pitching, 131
chains, rattling, 99
championship sports game, nationally televised, 139
cheese of power, rotting, xviii
chicken pox, magical, 64
chocolate factory, 128
Church of the Water-Day Saints, 116
cingulum, 74
circuses, 124
clam chlamydia, 64
cloak of invisibility, 76
community, wizarding, xv
Conceptual, Joncage the, 101
counter-spell, 144
counter-, 144
over-the-, 144
cricket, 130
crustacea, 57
crystals, deep shiny prettiness of, 78
cursed items, impropriety of disposing in the toilet, 83
damnation, 138, 143
dandekudzucrabliontigerrat-pigeons, 119
dark realm, dark, 81

Death
greeting cards sold by, 97
inevitability of, 97
different, magically. *See* magically different
Disembodied, Omniius the, xvii
divorce papers, 75
do-gooders and their ilk, 145
dominoes, ultimate, 131
domitae supernaturae, 56
double-blind studies, rigorous, 139
Dowsing Abuse Resistance Education, 46
dragonfire, 120
dragons, 65, 105, 119, 120
elephator, 118
elves, 107
lightweight, functional, 172
pet theories of, 29
specially trained, 172
Enchanted Persons, Registrar of, xv, 36
ability to capture evil sorcers without help from spunky young wizards, with or without mystical scars, 43
abnormality of, 150
duties, most important, 42
eagerness of to see every citizen fulfill his or her full potential, 45
eight freakish shames of, 152
limitation of authority to magical citizens, 39
three freakish hearts of, 152
two duties of, 37
two heads of, 37
enchantment taxes, 50–52
enormous conical hats, 75
every rule in this book, exception to just about, 2
eye of newt, xv
fabricante de magia negra, 144
faery/-ies. *See* fairy/-ies
Fair Trade, Wand of, 134
fairs, dark arts and witchcrafts, 124
fairy/-ies, 107
fairy godmothers, 112
Feldman, Simcha and Benyamin, vi
fire, more likely to sneeze, 104
flaming graffiti that only you can see, 136
flavors that only you can taste, garlicky, 136
fly, fruit, 62
forces, unholy, 23, 83, 86, 134, 135, 139, 143
freaks, 151
freedom, sudden disappearance of large copper statues of, 39
frippery, 151
fruits and vegetables, disturbingly shaped, 157

ghost camera, 91
ghost riders in the sky, 98
Gimbel's, 90
gipp, fourth, 131
giraffelion, 117
Gloves That Match Any Coat, 79
Gobstoppers, Everlasting, 79
golden ticket, 128
Government Manual for New Wizards
powerful protective enchantments upon, xviii
refusal of to teach you how to cast spells, 31
self-reference to, xv, xx
treatment within of topics given short shrift at magic academies, xv
weak brothiness of, 5
Grand Chief Poobah and Number-One All Day Sucker, 106
gravity, 26, 27, 98, 151
Great Dragon Riots, 120
Greeting of A Hundred Pitchforks, 86
griffin, 58
Grumbledor, Eugustus, xvii
guitar
air, 80
magic, 80
hairless, three-headed, barb-tailed, hook-billed devil chicks, hissing, 60
health insurance, 50, 99, 151
Hell
eternal flames of, 88
for atheists, 139
lack of fury within like a she-demon in a bad mood, 142
unholy fires of, 134
very stones of, 140
Hep, Calloway the, 101
Holy, Evander the, 132
horse, winged, 58
Human-Leprechaun Treaty o' 1743, 111
hydra, 62
hyperbole, 141
indelible ink, 142
Individual Reincarnation Account, 95
infinite loop, 144
influenza, 64
ITC Century Book, 12-point, 172
jewelry, magical, 77
Kennedy Centaur, 126
kleptomania, 64
knife. *See* athame
Kremlin, 100
Kutner, Rob, vi
l******************, a***c*****a, h**** p****, and SHAZA*!, 3*
Lands
Eight Shining, xix
Four in Need of Polishing, xix
language, gender-neutral, 142

late-blooming thirty-eight-year-old, 44
leprechauns, 107
levitation, 156
libraries, dusty, cobwebbed, 153
lies and half-truths, commingled with whole-truths, xx
Lincoln Centaur, 126
LUATHAR NOK RUATHA, 78
magic, mauve, 137
Magical Union of Tamers and Trainers, 61
magically different. *See* freaks
magician-at-law, 53, 54, 141
magie noir, la, 139
magikwondo, 131
Manipulator, Gorthodrex the, xix, 42
Melvin, He Who Must Not Be Named
    inadvertent contribution of to the fiscal stability of the MagicAlert bracelet industry, 77
    rumored theft of a powerful mystical item, 43
    undeniable benevolence of, 5
Mermanism, 116
metonymy, 141
mice, white magical, 57
mild indigestion, projectile, 156
minotaur disease, mad, 64
Misanthrope, Malcontento the, 82
mischievous younger brother. *See* younger brother, mischievous. *See also* Brozik, Wade
Molitor, Doug, vi
momentum, conservation of, 151
money, suitcase of, 131
Moore, Gregory the, vi
mudpits, 145
musky odor, 140
mysterious matters, discussed in hushed tones, 43
nattering, old spellhurler's, xx
Naturist, Narwhalg the, 151
New York Soul Exchange, 138
Noooooooooooo, 147
North Camelot, 129
oatmeal, perils of eating with salt instead of suger, xix
odors that reek of horribly decaying flesh, foul, 96
ogres, 107
Oiellet, 135
Oklahoma, 126
Old Country, 130
Omniius the Disembodied. *See* Disembodied, Omniius the
ophimonocleide, 79
Orb, Organic, 134
Orlando, 127
orphans, kidnapping, 137
parchment, dragon-skin, 172
participation, unwilling, 135
pegasus, 58

pharmacology, phantasmagorical, 50
phoenix, 58, 65
pin-up, 75
pit
  bull terriers, 68
  ducks, 68
  guinea pigs, 68
pitfalls, societal, of wizardry, xv
poltergeist, 96
Potion of Eternal Passion, 44
power cosmic, the, 145
power, limitless, 147
powers, eldritch, 151
Professor Shepard's Infinite Almanac, 118
projectile vomiting. *See* vomiting, projectile
prophesy fulfillment, ironic and painful, 156
prophets, false, 157
Push Me–Pull Ewe, 117
Push Me–Pull You, 117
Queen, Albino, xix, 42
quill, phoenix-feather, 172
rabbits, 32, 125, 127
  distaste for charms of, 33
  ears of, 32
  feet of, 32
rabies, 64
ragnanny, 131
ratiocination, involuntary, 38
rats of malfeasance and irresponsibility, twin, xviii
rattlepiranha, 119
recovering addicts, 151
Revolutionary, Lenin the, 100
Ring, Teme and Jeff, vi
roc, 65
romantic partner, long-term, 143
Rosiline, xvii
Sager Weinstein, Lauren, v
Sager, Dennis, Jeanni, Deborah, Michael, and Jill, vi
Sans Serifa, 172
Satan
  jokes of, 135
  likelihood that he is a bit of a jerk, 134
satyr, 140
scar, mundane, 170
scary fairies, wariness near, 69
Scrabble, Extreme, 131
seax. *See* yag-dirk
Secretary of the Treasury
  tendency of to reveal the fact that his name is Dimplestoutskin within an index, little suspecting that it will there be discovered by a resourceful young princess, 53
Shaagoth, 135
Shansky, Barbara, v

she-demon, 142
Shepard, Robert the, vi
Sherer, He Who Must Be Named
Melvyn, vi
Shih Who Must Be Named
Lucinda, vi
silverware, 39
Social Security numbers,
insuitability of for inscribing
upon swords, 73
something hideous, xvi
souvenir t-shirts, accursed, 81
spaying, neutering, and/or
de-sporulation, 62
Spell of Deception, 130
spellcasters of tomorrow, 149
spring day, beautiful, 139
squid, giant, 58
staffs, bad puns involving, 73
Staten Island Faery, 112
steam, magical, xv
stoning, 157
Supreme, Stewart the, 135
Swinging, Cugat the, 101
teenage wizards, 76
telephone, 35
television show, Sunday morning,
157
thaumo-tag, 45
tigers, 39
toe of bat, xv
Tooth Fairy, 112
trolls, 105
Turtlewolves, The Flying, 77
twoozer, 131
unicorn, 58
suitability of for wizards with
inflatable furniture, 59
unicorns, 105
universe, alternate, 40, 139
vampire, 87, 89, 90, 94
enslaving of, 92
popular sports among, 131
vampires, citizenship status of,
108
Vegetable Lamb of Tartary, 61
victims of natural disasters, 151
vision
any at all, 156
blurred, 156
clear, 156
vomiting, projectile, 156
wands, 72
war veterans, 151
Weinstein, Harris, Rosa, Josh,
Lisa, Simon, and Molly, vi
werewolves, 108
White, Elmar the, xvii
whooping crane cough,
magical, 64
Wise, Flegmar the, 94
witch doctors, 50
witch veterinarian, 62
wizarding schools, 76, 151

wizardolescence, 20–17
first experience of love during, 44
inimical and/or romantic feelings caused by, xx
wizards
nasty, lying, 150
Wizards Prison, 39, 40, 41, 149, 157
inexpensive but clean hotels near, 41
simultaneous ability and reluctance of guards to suck the life out of inmates of, 41
situation within Rahway, New Jersey, 40
World Wide Wizards Web, 76
www.governmentmanual.org, click here
yag-dirk. *See* knife
younger brother, mischievous, 172
youth, eternal, 147
Zohn, Sheryl, vi
zombies, 87
good conversation starters upon meeting, 89

ABOUT THE AUTHORS

Matthew David Brozik has a mundane scar on his forehead that is the result of an unenchanted childhood accident involving no black magic whatsoever. On the other hand, he does speak many curses, and believes that he lives a charmed life. His short fiction has appeared in such publications as the *Sycamore Review*, *Spout Magazine*, *Sidewalks*, *Barbaric Yawp*, and the *Dogwood Journal*. Not long before the publication of

The Government Manual for New Superheroes, Matthew left the practice of law to be a full-time writer of humor books, humorous novels, and short, semi-humorous autobiographical paragraphs. He lives in New York.

Photo: NATALIA SIMONS

Jacob Sager Weinstein lives in a magical land across the waves, populated by strange creatures such as "bobbies" and "solicitors." He lives backward in time, which means that his tendency to be late for deadlines is actually a sign of extreme punctuality. His work has appeared in *The Onion* (a statement that seems far more mysterious if you write the name of the magazine in non-italic, uncapitalized letters.) He is a former staff writer for *Dennis Miller Live* and a current staff wielder for the forces of good.

Photo: SIMCHA FELDMAN

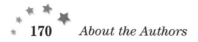

About the Typeface

Each copy of this book was individually inscribed on dragon-skin parchment with a phoenix-feather quill by a specially trained elf, making it impossible to say which typeface your particular copy will feature. If it was penned by the lightweight, functional elf known as Sans Serifa, it will likely be in 12-point ITC Century Book. If, however, it was penned by her mischievous younger brother, it will be in ITC Century Book disappea